# WINCHMORE

## MEMORIES
OF A
## LOST VILLAGE.

ILLUSTRATED

WITH LEAVES FROM

THE DOCTOR'S SKETCH BOOK.

By H. C.

SECOND EDITION. ALL RIGHTS RESERVED.

Republished by
SOUTHGATE CIVIC TRUST
November 1982

First published 1907
Reprinted January 1912.

Second Edition November 1912
THOMAS HUNTER, WATSON & CO LTD.,
DUMFRIES.

Republished by
SOUTHGATE CIVIC TRUST
November 1982
Printed in England
by Bowman Rocastle
Hertford

ISBN 0 905494 02 4

# CONTENTS.

| Chapter. | | Page. |
|---|---|---|
| | Preface to the Second Edition ... ... ... | 5 |
| | Introduction ... ... ... ... ... | 7 |
| I. | Fifty Years Ago ... ... ... ... ... | 9 |
| II. | In the Village ... ... ... ... ... | 14 |
| III. | Sketches :— | |
| | 1. Elder Blossom ... ... ... ... | 21 |
| | 2. A Carriage Accident ... ... ... | 22 |
| | 3. The Comet of 1858 ... ... ... | 23 |
| | 4. The Building of the Schools ... ... | 24 |
| | 5. A Walk by the New River ... ... | 26 |
| | 6. The Hailstorm ... ... ... ... | 30 |
| | 7. The Cart on the Green ... ... ... | 31 |
| | 8. Esprit de Corps ... ... ... ... | 33 |
| | 9. The Velocipede ... ... ... ... | 35 |
| | 10. Old-Fashioned Toy Dogs ... ... | 38 |
| | 11. China Asters ... ... ... ... | 39 |
| | 12. Cakes, &c. ... ... ... ... | 42 |
| IV. | Birds' Nests ... ... ... ... ... | 45 |
| V. | Reminiscences ... ... ... ... ... | 51 |
| VI. | The Wood ... ... ... ... ... | 62 |
| VII. | The Hiving of the Bees ... ... ... ... | 68 |
| VIII. | Round by the World's End ... ... ... | 78 |
| IX. | Ford's Grove Cottage ... ... ... ... | 90 |
| X. | Some Former Inhabitants ... ... ... | 96 |
| XI. | Chiefly Historical ... ... ... ... | 100 |
| XII. | The Coming of the Railway ... ... ... | 110 |
| XIII. | A Lay of the Suburbs ... ... ... ... | 116 |

# PREFACE, 1982

Seventy-five years have passed since Henrietta Cresswell's *Winchmore Hill: Memories of a Lost Village* first appeared in print. During that time Winchmore Hill has undergone changes far more extensive than those observed by Miss Cresswell during her 46 years' residence in the village.

I am glad that it has now proved possible to reprint this delightful little book. To anyone who knows Winchmore Hill, it provides a fascinating glimpse of life in the village before the encroachment of suburbia.

The second edition, published in November 1912, has been chosen for the reprint. This was longer and more copiously illustrated than the first edition, published in 1907 and reprinted in January 1912. Both editions have now become collectors' items.

The book was published after Miss Cresswell moved away from Winchmore Hill to settle in Dumfries in 1900. From there she moved to Watermillock, on Ullswater, in 1920, and died there in 1931 at the age of 77. Her father's sketches and watercolours, some of which illustrate this book, are an equally precious record of the old village. Fortunately, many of them have been preserved and are now cared for by the London Borough of Enfield.

PETER HODGE
*Winchmore Hill*
*September 1982*

# PREFACE TO THE SECOND EDITION.

The First Edition of this little book being out of print, I have been asked by many people to republish it; and I hope this issue will be found better than its predecessor.

I was requested to tell what I knew of Fords Grove Cottage when it was still a " cottage of gentility," and have also added a short chapter of other memories.

I must call attention to the fact that any discrepancies in dates are accounted for by my original MS. having been written several years ago. When it was first published I was begged to make no alterations in it.

It is now seventy years since my Father first came to Winchmore Hill. One portrait shows what he was then like, and the other is from a photograph, taken by my brother Francis, about two years before his death.

I believe the sketch of the old wooden cottages near the " King's Head " to have been one of the first he made. They were some of the oldest and most picturesque in the place. Another view looking west towards Hill House has been chosen for the cover.

Few places have altered more than Middle Lane. The drawing placed as Frontispiece must have been made previous to 1860. In the other view, looking towards the village, the wooden stable on the left marks the site of the present St. Paul's Church Institute.

In view of the great changes now taking place in Winchmore Hill Wood, two drawings have been reproduced, showing the footpath near the Keeper's Cottage and the gate entering the Village.

The view of the old " Retreat " seems of particular interest now that a whole town has sprung up between " Old Green Dragon Lane " and Enfield.

Hoppers Road has been greatly altered during the last ten or twelve years.

The small pencil drawing of Ford's Grove House, in the Green Lanes, is a great contrast to the present High Road with its tramways.

The old " King's Head " will be a new view to many people.

The sketch in the Green Lanes near the Cock Tavern, though not in Winchmore Hill, appears to me of considerable interest.

I may mention that my Grandmother Cresswell's pet name for me was " Winifred."

I must thank many kind friends for their letters about my book, which it has given me the greatest pleasure to receive.

Henrietta Cresswell.

Nunholm House, Dumfries,
    November, 1912.

# INTRODUCTION.

My father, John Cresswell, was a general practitioner at Winchmore Hill for fifty years, from 1842 till his death on November 9th, 1892. When he came he was a young man of 24, and he only slept away from home twice or thrice for a single night in more than forty years. There can only be a few people now who remember " The Old Doctor," but there was a time when he brought nearly every new inhabitant into the village, and saw most of the old ones out.

In his time the somewhat primitive village developed into a considerable suburb, and in the fifteen years since his passing away it has become a modern wilderness of bricks and mortar, and has been " improved " nearly out of existence.

His sketch book was always in his hand and his drawing minutely accurate in detail. I hope some of the many dwellers in the new village may be interested in his sketches of the old, now passed away into " The Land of Long Ago." I have attempted in a few chapters of word painting to give some idea of how we lived in Winchmore Hill in those days. I have made my sketches as true to life as I was able, and have done my best not to be too egotistical.

If I have failed in this I crave forgiveness.

Henrietta Cresswell.

Dumfries, 1907.

*Middle Lane about 1860 (now Station Road)*

## CHAPTER I.

## FIFTY YEARS AGO.

Winchmore Hill half a century ago was a small village ten miles from London, away from the high road, on the outskirts of the district known as Enfield Chase.

If you mentioned its name a few miles away your hearer was often ignorant of its very existence. It was in the depths of the country, and is nearly unrecognisable in the flourishing suburb of to-day. To get to it from London you took the omnibus from the " Flower Pot " in Bishopsgate Street. The omnibus has vanished; the Flower Pot has vanished, gone with the London of Dickens, and surely Winchmore Hill has vanished—gone into the " Land of Long Ago." No, the old village has not quite disappeared; even now there are unchanged corners, and houses that have stood a hundred and fifty or two hundred years.

At the Flower Pot you would have found the " Little Wonder " with the old coachman on the box, and the conductor on the step waiting for its passengers.

A few years earlier when the Doctor first came to the Village there was a stage-coach, which carried Her Majesty's Mails once a day to the " Green Dragon," where the villagers called for their letters. The return fare was five shillings, but the " Little Wonder " justified its name by performing the journey twice daily, at the cost of only half-a-crown.

There was not over-much hurry in starting, the yellow paint shone in the misty London sunshine, the brown horse and the old blue roan were at the pole, there was a crack of the whip and a straining at the traces and the omnibus rattled away in the pride of novelty and progress, over the bumpy granite pavement of Bishopsgate, through Norton Folgate, past the " Eastern Counties " Railway Station at Shoreditch, along Kingsland, to the more open country of Stamford Hill, till the fine old elms at Tottenham, called the "Seven Sisters," came in sight. The village of Tottenham clustered round its large green, and the ivy-mantled tower of the old Church was visible in mid-distance among the trees across the fields, the Grammar School and High Cross were passed, the houses became fewer, many of them standing back from the road in beautiful gardens.

The omnibus reached Edmonton, passing the old " Bell " Inn, with the very balcony from which Mrs Gilpin cried so franctically to honest John, as he galloped madly and helplessly away towards Ware, or anywhere. It is the custom to mock at John Gilpin's horsemanship, but he must have had a good seat to stick to the Calendar's horse for so many miles. Ware is a good deal more than " full ten miles off " from Edmonton, it is much nearer fifteen. At the " Angel," a short distance further on, the 'bus turned westward along Silver Street. At that time the road to the east, opposite the " Angel," was picturesque in the extreme, and was rightly named Water Lane; in wet weather it was more a river than a road, on its south side was a row of dilapidated cottages on a high causeway, and on the other bank of the stream was a solitary white house with a tiled roof, sheltered by a tree and reached by a row of stepping stones and a steep wooden ladder.

Silver Street led to the " Highlands " of Winchmore Hill and Southgate, as they were called by the folk of the Lea Marshes. It was bounded on the right by the palings of Pym's Park, and further on by the wide Pym's Brook, over-

## WINCHMORE HILL.

hung by trees, and blossoming in summer with yellow waterlilies, on the left were wooden cottages with gay gardens. Near the " Black Bull " at the hamlet of Tanner's End, the turning to the Workhouse was passed, at Wyerhall was a lovely corner, with a ford, a footbridge, and overhanging foliage, and then the country opened out to the corn fields and pastures of Huxley Farm.

The Windmill, standing alone at the end of a field half-a-mile across, was a landmark from all around, and the rich alluvial soil forming the pre-historic bed of the river Lea, which is said to have been a great river when the Thames was a mere streamlet, grew wheat and crops such as no stiff clay or harsh gravel could produce.

Firs Lane and Hedge Lane, as the continuation of Silver Street was called, made an angle where the great rick yards of Huxley Farm stood beside the low house covered with creepers. At one end of the house was a conservatory—a place of beauty on which to gaze through the iron railings. When the trees were bare and snow on the ground there was a wonderland of waxen camelias, scarlet and white with glossy green leaves; but in summer the lane itself held flowers enough and to spare, not only to long for, but to gather freely in handfuls. Honeysuckle and wild hops clambered over the hedges round the stackyard, wild roses were on both sides of the way. White briony and black briony draped the quickset with festoons of greenery. A bend in the streamlet formed a small pond full of forget-me-nots, and the sides of the road on the hill to the New River bridge were rich with lush grass, on which some gipsy boys were pasturing the horse of the basket woman's van.

At that time there was a pathway along the banks of the New River which might be followed for miles. The black gates and the Catherine wheel fences were placed there later.

The tired horses dragged the omnibus slowly up the steep bridge, and then settled down to a steady trot as they neared Palmer's Green, a small triangle of grass, where the green lanes were crossed. At the corner was a large pond, with white railings and dipping steps, where some boys were fishing for stickle-backs, so gaudily scarlet and green in their wedding finery. On the right, as Hoppers Road was entered, stood a row of cottages with long gardens. Next to them was Eaton Farm with old barns roofed with antique mossy tiles. At the turning by the " Dog and Duck " Southgate passengers alighted, having only a mile to walk by the lane to Bourne Hill, locally known as " The Bone." A carrier's cart standing between the small public-house and a pond, made the roadway almost too narrow for the larger vehicle to pass. Then the leafy vista of Hoppers Road came in view, with the first cottages of the Hill in the distance. It was a beautiful road. On the left were pines and larches, beeches and oaks, old forest land and newer plantations, the unspoilt virgin woodland of Enfield Chase. There were trees that were centuries old, and even the fields were full of fine timber. The hedgerows were bowers of hawthorn, a perfect snowstorm of bloom in May time. An old garden was passed, and on one of the trees was a board with the blood-curdling notice—" Mantraps and Spring Guns are set here." Then there was one of the many low verandah-fronted houses of the neighbourhood. The Little Wonder stopped at the gates of Highfield Park, where a fine avenue stretched away to the house. A peacock was strutting up and down, and circling slowly round to display the glories of his expanded tail. " Aunt " Bury, the gatekeeper, came out of the hexagonal thatched lodge for a parcel she had been expecting. The peacock was full of hope when he saw her, and a flock of

## WINCHMORE HILL.

white turkeys came forward hastily to know if it were feeding time.

The heavy iron gates clanked to, and the horses strained at their collars to start afresh. A row of tall Lombardy poplars were passed, and then the Doctor's house, where the scent of the sweet-briar hedge mingled with the fragrance of climbing roses. Next door stood a white brick chapel. On the opposite side was the carrier's yard and some cottages, and then the horses breasted the short hill into the village— a little old-fashioned country place, a green where boys played cricket and rounders, and a round pond encircled with willows, on which a flock of ducks were swimming. Some geese were preening their feathers on the grass by the pump, where some of the village folk were waiting their turn with buckets, most of them gay-coloured American pails made of wood with iron handles. On the stretch of turf below the pond a boy was washing a cart. From a deep entry leading to the blacksmith's forge, the ring of the hammer on the anvil sounded through the still air.

The gabled weather-boarded cottage and bakehouse which stood at the corner of the Hoppers Road had a garden full of flowers. In spring the great cherry tree that overhung the footpath was a mass of white blossom, and in late summer beds of clove carnations filled the air with perfume.

The 'bus rumbled through the village and halted at the " King's Head," where the passengers who lived on the Hill alighted, and then took its way a half-mile further to its stables at the " Green Dragon," in the Green Lanes. It took nearly two hours to reach Winchmore Hill from the City, as it was such an out-of-the-way corner of the world.

There was a tradition among the old folk of the village that it was made last thing on Saturday night out of the rubbings of the pan.

## CHAPTER II.

### IN THE VILLAGE.

The old gabled house between the village pond and Hoppers Road was the baker's. It was very picturesque, built of weather-boarding and roofed with mossy tiles, and had an extensive yard and huge barns and granaries. There was a bakehouse of the old sort with an oven heated by burning faggots within, and there were long kneading troughs under the window. White and purple lilac lined the fence of the yard. At one end near the gates stood the tall sign of the " Salisbury Arms," and at the top of Compton Lane was a triangle of grass, a fenced-in shrubbery of straggling hawthorn bushes, and a fine horse chestnut tree in full bloom. At one time Mr and Mrs Burns had the bakehouse, but they moved to the Farm near the Doctor's to keep dairy cows, and turned all their attention to milk instead of bread. Mrs Burns made hay herself, in the field with the oak trees beyond the carrier's garden, and she made it with a hay fork of her very own, with handle painted in alternate lengths of red and green. Oh, that hay fork! Little Winifred, the Doctor's daughter, thought it very nice to turn over the sweet hay with a forked stick, cut for her by her father, but how she longed for that scarlet and green implement! At last there came a glorious hour when the good-natured Quakeress lent it to her to use herself. She felt that if ever she had a field of her own she would have a fork exactly like that and her hay would be all the sweeter. Mrs Burns made butter in a churn, and Winifred learned to turn the handle slowly round while the cream went swish, swish. In time the swish became a

*The Wood Gate, looking towards the Village.*

## WINCHMORE HILL.

duller sound and the churn turned more heavily. After that there came a feeling of something flop, flopping, and behold, there was the golden yellow butter ! It was very interesting making butter in a bottle, only it was so difficult to get the butter out of it when it was done; but to use a real churn was something to be proud of.

Before Mrs Burns had the baker's shop the two Miss Catchpoles owned the business. They, like the Burns', belonged to the Society of Friends. Friend Lydia and her sister kept bees, and kept them most successfully. They had so much honey they hardly knew how to use it, so it occurred to their minds to make some mead. They appear to have imagined that it was, what we should now call a temperance drink, a sort of *eau sucrée* of the most harmless nature. One cold winter's evening as they sat over the fire they thought they would try their new brew. It was certainly very good. The sister retired early, but Friend Lydia felt so cosy by the fire that she had another glass. She had never felt better in her life, but when she awoke in the grey wintry morning in her armchair with the fire out and the cold grey ashes looking dismal and forlorn, amazement entered her soul. When she met the Doctor next day she told him about it, and how good the mead had tasted, but added she, " I fear, Friend John, I must have been *powerfully refreshed."*

There was another gabled wooden house on the north side of the green, and it was a very peculiar dwelling, as it was not built on ordinary foundations, but stood on a framework resting upon wheels. It was a long low cottage with two or three gables facing the road. The wheels were heavy discs of wood, sunk in a flower border to the axletrees, and it is said that its first owner intended to remove when he wished, house and all, as they now do in America, but alas, in an unlucky moment he (or was it she) planted a row of lime trees in front of it, and by law those trees could not be cut down without permission from the landlord, and the house could not be removed while the trees obstructed the way, so it remained a " Tenant's Fixture," not in the usual sense of the word, in spite of the wheels, until Suburbia improved it off the face of the earth.

On the east side of this cottage a low ceiled archway led to the blacksmith's forge, and westward was the " King's Head " garden, where lavender and rosemary and white pinks flourished, and where there was a pond, on which floated waxen water lilies. In spring the rent oak fence by the roadside was overhung with white and purple lilacs and guelder roses—Whitsun bosses, as they were called. At the corner opposite the King's Head a huge walnut tree overshadowed the footpath.

The old Inn, with its small window panes, was built long enough ago to have seen many changes. The square white house on the south side of the pond had a large garden and fields, which reached down Middle Lane to the back of the Queen's Head. There were several cows and an old piebald pony, said to have been in work for thirty years. At one time the cows were in good milk, and yet morning after morning, one or the other was dry. It was evident some one was stealing the milk, and the village constable was set to watch, but without any result. The mysterious loss continued, and Mr Feltham, who lived in the white house, grew more and more annoyed. At last some kind neighbour hinted that he would be wise to watch the watcher. He did so, and in the early dawn of the next day, greatly to his delight, he caught the thief in the act—the honest policeman was milking the cows himself.

On the west side of the green, near where the road goes up to the Wood gate, was a large and important shop. In

*Ford's Grove House, from Middle Lane.
The Cottage may be seen in the distance.*

*The Old "King's Head," 1860.*

## WINCHMORE HILL.

the old days " Udall's " was well known for many miles around. Travellers' carts took drapery and haberdashery to all the county houses and villages. People were frugal in those days. One year the Doctor's wife, the Brewer's wife, the Stockbroker's wife, and the Papermaker's sister would all appear clothed from the same length of material, and the following summer the junior members of each family appeared in the remainders of the garments. There was not much variety in the old shop. The Doctor's wife would take a piece of stuff she had purchased two or three years before to be matched, and if there was a delay in finding it, would point to the shelves and say calmly, " I had it from the second box on the third shelf," and there, sure enough, it would be found. On one occasion some alterations were made in the building, and stores of foreign laces and silks were discovered hidden in a secret place, long forgotten. No doubt, they had been there since the old smuggling days. Enfield Chase was a wild and lawless land, and Udall's, an easy stage from London, and only a few miles from the Essex Marshes, was a convenient place for the pack-horses to stop unquestioned.

At Christmas the mistress of the shop made a beautiful entertainment with a fine Christmas tree, and sometimes a conjurer, to which were invited the children of her customers, in and near the village. These parties were great events to Winifred, and she enjoyed them far more than many grander affairs of later date.

The old village was a primitive place. In a little low house near the forge was a school—not a mere dame school, but a select day school for boys and girls. It was decidedly a liberal Academy, at which the sons and daughters of the butcher, the baker, and candlestick-maker learnt their Christ-cross row with those of the class above them. Winifred only went there for breaking-up parties and great festivities, but she learnt some wonderful facts which had been taught to the other scholars; for instance that the climate of Central Africa is so hot that all the natives have to do to *heat their flat irons* is to stand them out in the sun. It was the custom of the little girls to bring flowers to their teacher. Emily and Marien from the nursery garden brought a rose bud and a spray of maidenhair fern. Medora from Fillcap's Farm brought some sweet peas and mignonette, and each bouquet had a piece of silver paper wrapped neatly round the stems. Winifred's cousin from Devonshire felt it behoved her to follow the fashion, and begged her grandmother for a nosegay; and a nosegay she had. Such a beaupot as never was seen. All the best the garden could produce—and such a garden! It was no meagre offering but a real Cook's bunch. Some of its chief glories were oriental poppies and huge white peonies. It was a proud child who bore it to school, but at the moment of making the gift she was covered with confusion. All the stems were naked and unashamed, the decent covering of tissue paper having been forgotten, and every girl in the school was sniggering at the gaudy vulgarity of the glorious blossoms, and mentally comparing them with their own refined little button-holes. No doubt, Miss T. appreciated her present at its true value, for the grandmother's garden was well known to fame. In that garden was an enormous weeping ash. One lady visitor, who was over strong in her " h's," spent half an afternoon expressing her admiration of the " hash harbour." At the end of the garden was a tall yew tree, which may still be seen behind the houses near Vicar's Moor Railway Bridge.

Before Miss T. had the school old Miss Watkins was the mistress, and on the day the Prince of Wales (King Edward VII.) was married, she gave a party. The Doctor's wife, who was ill at the time, sat up in bed to make a most

## WINCHMORE HILL.

refined little wedding favour for Winifred to wear—a white satin bow with a spray of myrtle and orange blossom from her own wedding wreath; but, alas, its glories paled and withered into home-made simplicity when it was side by side with the gay red, white, and blue rosettes with gold or silver Prince-of-Wales' feathers in the centre worn by the other young ladies. The crowning glory of that day was the first sight of an Air Balloon. It floated into sight high in the blue sky in the far south, beyond the pond and the willows, beyond the old bakehouse—a pear-shaped ball turning slowly as it travelled in the cold March air. The news that it was in sight spread quickly, and groups of villagers and children gazed open-mouthed while it showed now pale pink, and now blue and iridescent, in the afternoon light like mother-of-pearl. It passed steadily westward till it disappeared beyond the trees of the wood, " lost to sight, to memory dear."

Near the " Salisbury Arms " was a tiny shop kept by two ancient spinsters, the Misses Lowen. One of them was quite deaf, and as bald as an egg—a rather forbidding old lady from whom to make purchases. The other had no legs! She travelled on her hands down the two steps from the small back parlour and along the floor behind the counter, and there raised herself acrobatically on to a high stool to serve customers. She wore a most palpable front kept in place by a band of black velvet across the forehead. She was a kind old lady, and a favourite with children. The Misses Lowen sold tobacco, snuff, short clay pipes, and long churchwardens. There were also various primitive toys, Dutch dolls and Paradise dolls, and long snakes made of horn turnings, with black bead eyes and red cloth tongues, which were packed quite small in conical wooden boxes. They kept beads and marbles, stoneys at twenty a penny, and glass allys at a whole farthing a-piece, boxes of dominoes, hoops and hoop sticks, and stocks of tin whistles.

The Doctor attended these old ladies entirely for the price of his tobacco, giving each time a curiously twisted note which represented payment.

## CHAPTER III.

### SKETCHES.

#### 1.—ELDER BLOSSOM.

It was Coronation Day, and the great elder bushes in the carrier's garden were a mass of bloom. It was the Doctor's wedding day. His wife said that though there were no bells at St. James', Pentonville, where she was married, every bell in London should ring, so she chose Coronation Day. She waited twelve years for the Doctor, and told her friends it was better waiting for something than nothing, and on the 28th of June, 1852, she came home to Winchmore Hill. The journey from London was made in a post-chaise, with a pair of white horses and a postilion, and when she saw the elder bushes she called them her wedding bouquets. She was welcomed home to the house opposite to them, and could look from her window over the cluster roses and sweet-briar hedge to the road. Beyond were the holly trees and the elders, and a May-duke cherry tree loaded with fruit in the carrier's garden, then a large field with oak trees and the deep green of the wood. While she was thinking of the elder bushes and the joy bells, and rejoicing in being home at last in the quiet country so far from smoky London, the post-chaise was rumbling away to its stables at Colney Hatch, and in the boot was all the family plate, the wedding presents of old silver, forgotten in the excitement of the arrival. It was not missed till it was too late to do anything, so it remained all night in the boot of the chaise under a shed in an open livery stable yard, whence it was rescued next morning by the Doctor's sister, who had tramped three miles to fetch it, and three miles home again, bearing the heavy portmanteau in triumph.

## 2.—A CARRIAGE ACCIDENT.

Winifred was taken to town by the Doctor to visit her grandmother. She was a tiny child, less than three years old, but the journey was so eventful that it was impressed on her memory for ever. There was no " railroad train " on the Great Northern line nearer than Hornsey Station, so a perambulator was borrowed, the little maid tucked into it, and the journey began. It was hot and fine and dusty. The Doctor always walked fast, and when he had gone a mile and a half he got very thirsty. He was not in the least accustomed to wheeling a perambulator, and it was a heavy little vehicle. At the " King's Arms " Bridge he halted, leaving the " pram " on the crest of the rise while he went to quench his thirst at the New River. He knelt down on the grass, leaning over the water and making a cup of his hand and rejoiced in the cool freshness of the drink. Presently there was a rattle and a crash, and a pitiful voice calling " Papa, papa," and to his horror he beheld the carriage resting on its handles with the front wheel high in the air, and the small Winifred head downwards in the roadway. He had put the vehicle so near to the top of the slope that the child's weight had completely overbalanced it as she turned her head over her shoulder to look after him. However, she was quite unhurt and very little frightened. No further event occurred all the way to Hornsey, where the chaise was safely left at the railway station for the return journey. A joyful day was spent, but she remembered nothing of her drive back to Winchmore Hill, for she slept all the way.

## WINCHMORE HILL.                                    23

### 3.—THE COMET OF 1858.

In the quiet life of the village small events were important, but in the coming and going of cottage, field, farm, and garden, the happenings of the great world of London seemed a long way away. News arrived by the mid-day omnibus. Great events were shouted by the driver as he passed, but they only rippled the calm surface of the village pond and were forgotten. Old Moore's Almanack was earnestly consulted for its weather prophecies, and great faith placed in them, but many were the head shakings over the advent of the Great Comet. On a calm Summer evening the Mother had walked part of the way to Hornsey with her brother from London. Her little daughter Winifred was with her. They halted on the " King's Arms " Bridge over the New River, a short distance from the " Cock " at Bowes Farm, to say good-bye. It was a lovely evening—the sky amber and aquamarine. Grey mists were creeping up from the winding silver ribbon of water and the willow-shrouded banks of Pym's Brook. The dark yew trees made a black mass in front of the weird old white house known as Bowes Farm, and contrasted with the bright afterglow in the Western sky. The evening star burnt palely in the heavens, and cast a quivering reflection into the rippling water beneath. A candle in a window of the gable roofed " Cock Inn " made a point of light. The " King's Arms " which gave the name to the bridge had already ceased to exist. The site was occupied by a nursery garden, and a faint perfume of mignonette mingled with the evening air. The scene was peace itself. The silence was only broken by the last chipper of a bird in the elm trees or the splash of a fish jumping in the river, but above and beyond all else, dominating the light, the silence, and the landscape, was the first sight of the

Great Comet, small as yet, and appearing as a bright star and a strange, ever-widening beam of light paling the planets by contrast. That was the first time Winifred saw it, but after, night by night, it grew till half the sky seemed full of the glory of it, and then when it had become part of her young life, it decreased as it had increased and was gone. The village was left with only the Comet year as a date to reckon by. Many regarded it with awe, and even with terror, but no memory of it remained to Winifred in after life so distinct as that of the first sight of its glory, over the fields, the stream, and the slow flowing river on that night so long ago.

### 4.—THE BUILDING OF THE SCHOOLS.

At one time in the life of the village events were referred to as having taken place in " the year of the Fancy Fair." The Fair—it was not called a Bazaar—was got up to raise funds for the building of the National Schools. Up to that time a one-roomed cottage on Church Hill had fulfilled the educational wants of the neighbourhood, but was quite inadequate for modern requirements. A Committee of Improvement was formed, and a great effort made, with the result that large new buildings were erected close to the Church, upon a site given by the Proprietor of the Wood.

The Fair was a great event. The weather was perfect, and the neighbouring inhabitants flocked *en masse* to the beautiful park in which it was held. To Winifred it was the greatest festivity she had ever known, and she had all the excitement of wearing a new hat and driving quite a long way in Newby's fly to the Lodge gates on Bourne Hill, and into the park, where the deer crowded together in alarm among the trees. There were large white tents and flags, a band playing martial airs, crowds of people, carriages and

*Hopper's Road, looking South.*

## WINCHMORE HILL.

horses, and a beautiful lake with islands reflected in its calm waters. The Doctor had written verses suitable to the occasion, and they were really in print. He had also painted views of the village at the top of sheets of notepaper that were almost equal to the copper-plate engravings of Margate and Sandgate, upon which the Mother wrote letters when she went to the seaside. The Doctor's sister had performed miracles of needlework in Berlin wool work, and fish scales and feathers. She had made a whole set of dinner mats in feather work that were perfect in the harmony of their colouring, but somewhat lacking in suitability from a purely practical point of view. Everyone in the village had worked their hardest, and the stalls were full of a wonderful collection of goods of all sorts. Winifred became the happy possessor of a real live Jack-in-the-box. A box covered with marbled paper and a Jack with a fiery red beard. The Mother on the second day, when things became cheap, bought a pair of Ormolu candlesticks with crystal drops that could be unhung and held up to the light for you to look through the prisms and see all the colours of the rainbow. They were a joy for many a day. The years numbered three times seven before there was another Bazaar in Winchmore Hill, so it is little wonder that folk spoke of " the year of the Fancy Fair."

The schools were considered palatial. A narrow room sixty feet long with a high timbered roof and warmed by two fireplaces, a large infant school with galleries, spacious classrooms, and large playgrounds, undoubtedly an enormous advance on the one-roomed cottage on the side of the hill. The school stood in an angle of the wood. In Winter the wind whistled through the bare boughs, and the twigs broke under the weight of snow or glittered with all the needles of hoar frost. In Spring the birds sang from morning till night, and the cuckoo called as he flew over the playground. In Summer there was cool shade from the oak saplings which grew up to the very walls, and in the Autumn golden red and brown leaves made a glory against the blue sky and a many-coloured carpet for the feet of the children at play. It was in 1859 that the yellow brick buildings were completed, and they were opened with a grand concert, and wreaths of evergreens and mottoes of leaves on scarlet flannel backgrounds were made by the score to decorate the plain walls. Winifred was kept busy the whole morning sewing leaves on cardboard letters. She was only four years old, but could do something with her needle. She longed to see the decorations, but the concert was only for grown-up people, so the Doctor took her out with him as a make up.

### 5.—A WALK BY THE NEW RIVER.

Winifred and the Doctor went down Highfield Row for him to visit a sick child in " the Rookery " at the back of " the Orange Tree." It was a house where the stair was steep, and the ceiling so low that the Doctor invariably broke the top of his chimney-pot hat when he went there. He kept a little wooden trumpet in that hat which was rather a mystery. It was firmly wedged across the crown. Also he often came home with it full of flowers—cottage roses or clove pinks, or even a few mushrooms picked in a field as he went along. It was no wonder to the children that a person as clever as a conjurer should be able to produce live rabbits, packets of sweets, or miles of tissue paper ribbon out of a hat, as even the Doctor's served him always as a sort of light-weight pocket for sundries.

Why are so many inns called the " Orange Tree?" Was it out of compliment to Dutch Billy, I wonder? The

## WINCHMORE HILL.

Hostelry in Highfield Row was rather picturesque, with a round bow window of small panes, and with benches in the porch. The swinging signboard opposite stood on the edge of a running brook full of water-cress and forget-me-nots, with a golden border of fleabane on the bank. The rushes were long and green, and it was possible to get fine lengths of their velvety white pith. There were a dozen half-grown ducklings splashing in the water, and Winifred was too young to connect them mentally with the rows of green peas with well-filled pods in the garden next to the " Orange Tree." There was another " Orange Tree " at Colney Hatch, which place she believed was peopled entirely by lunatics, and there was a " Cherry Tree " at Southgate. She walked there with the Mother sometimes, but it was a long way. They always laid in a store of luscious brown gingerbread as a support by the way. It was bought at Ostcliffe's, by the Wood gate. The way lay through the Wood by the public path, past the keeper's cottage, over the stile by the cottages at Clappers Green to the Pound, where you might see a lean donkey or a plaintive calf awaiting the claim of their owners, then over another stile into the " Cherry Tree " fields and by the Mall to Southgate. In the fields at the path side stood an enormous elm with a huge trunk and knotty roots that made natural seats. That was where the gingerbread was always eaten, and for a long time Winifred fully believed that this was " the Cherry Tree " from which the fields were named.

The Doctor's patient in the Rookery had typhus fever, so the child was told to walk to the other side of the road till he had a good blow in the fresh air. She ran on before to the steep bridge over the New River where the cottagers came to dip all their water. More than once had a heavy bucket overbalanced some youthful Gibeonite, and he had fetched water no more. There was a footpath by the side of the river in those days, and a pleasant walk it made. It was delicious that hot afternoon to be on the cool turf and look down into the clear, deep water. There was a garden of waterweeds, among which could be seen the five black bars and the orange red fins and tail of a perch. He had his high back spine erected like the weapons of the company of the spearmen. His tail lapped gently to the slow-flowing water, and he cocked one eye knowingly at the shoal of silver bleak on the surface above him. They were snapping lazily at flies and water beetles. Close under the bank were minnows, and deep in mud where you seldom caught a glimpse of them lay the gudgeon, very like the bleak in shape, but more mud-coloured and wearing moustachios. If you looked into the dark pool under the bridge you might have the luck to see the shadowy form of a Jack nearly as large as Jonah's whale, or if the big fish was not at home, there might be seen the olive green back and red fins of a chub. Out in the sun, where the river bottom was gravelly, the Doctor pointed out a bull-head or miller's thumb between two large stones with his ridiculously small tail wagging behind. There was a small shoal of roach, silver, green, and ruby coloured, as they passed and re-passed in the sunshine. Isaac Walton called the carp the fox among the fishes, from his cunning ways, and the roach the sheep from its stupidity, but they are really very clever people, and the slightest shadow falling on the water makes them vanish entirely. There were some dace also near the Hedge Lane embankment, but they were pure silver with no jewellery, which made them much more difficult to see. Eyes get accustomed to the under water world, and many a person would stand on the river bridge and say they saw nothing of the life below the surface, while to another the old stream from Amwell was literally a book wherein he who stood still might read many things. The walk by the river was a great treat, because the Doctor knew all there was to know, and could tell it all. There was a dark form with great claws and an armour-plated tail like a small lobster which he said was a cray fish. It is only at times that they come into the open as their homes are in holes in the banks. The boys of Highfield Row sometimes caught whole baskets full by dragging a piece of raw meat tied to a string under the grass edges in the dusk of the evening. Soon the bed of the river became shallower and the sides more shelving, and there were curious looking shellfish standing end up in the sandy mud each waving his " foot "—a very odd sort of foot—in the air, or rather in the water, and the shells were gaping nearly half-an-inch apart, but the moment the Doctor's stick approached them each closed with a snap, and a row of bubbles floated to the surface above them. When he lifted three or four out on the bank they looked almost as solid as stones. He gathered some water weed and placed them with it in his red silk pocket handkerchief, knotted the corners together, and undertook to carry the treasures home. Tired, but proud and happy, Winifred plodded solemnly by his side along Hoppers Road. The fresh-water mussels were placed in a large pudding basin and some oatmeal scattered in the water to feed them. The home aquarium stood on the Mother's plant table near the window, but alas, their doom was sealed. He who finds some mischief still for idle hands to do bestowed on Winifred a piece of bright magenta coloured ribbon, quite the new colour and very gay. By accident an end of it dipped into the basin of water and a rosy rivulet sank slowly among the shells and stones at the bottom of the bowl. Winifred was fascinated. More ribbon was wetted and gently squeezed, and finally the whole remnant lay like a crimson snake in the water, which was dyed a bright magenta, as beautiful as the bottles in a chemist's shop window; but alas, next morning all the shells were wide open and the mussels lay dead in the crimson flood.  *Sic transit gloria mundi.*

## 6.—THE HAILSTORM.

It was high Summer, July, 1859. A hard and white winter had passed away, followed by a Spring in which the wealth of blossom had again clothed the fruit trees with snow. The world was full of promise, the corn stood thickly on the land, and trees were laden with fruit, the sultry heat of the weather was making life a burden. The morning sky had a lurid gleam and thunder muttered in the distance and rolled nearer and nearer as the day wore on. At mid-day the sky darkened to the tint of a Winter afternoon; the storm came closer and soon hail began to fall. Hail as large as peas, hail like marbles, hail the size of pigeon's eggs. The rattling on the window panes was deafening. " I will close the shutters," said the Mother, and even while she was doing so the glass fell shattered at her feet. Larger and larger grew the lumps of ice and the lightning flashed. It resembled the plague of Egypt, " Hailstones and Coals of Fire." The thunder in crashing peals shook the very foundations of the house, but could hardly be heard above the sounds of breaking glass and the hammering of the hailstones on the window shutters. The noise and the darkness appeared to last for hours, but all things have an end, and the time came when it was possible to go outside and venture into unshuttered rooms to see what the storm had done. In the upper chambers heaps of ice-lumps were piled against the wall opposite the window, which were swept up and carried away in shovels full. There was scarcely a whole pane of glass left in the

## WINCHMORE HILL. 31

west front of the house. The great " Reine Claude " greengage, the pride of the garden, had its fruit cut to pieces— sliced as with knives, the leaves were torn from the branches and many boughs broken, the flower beds were devastated. In the front garden the great arbutus tree was beaten to pieces as if with a flail, it never really recovered from the damage, and soon after died. It was so large a tree that its trunk was used in later years as a chopping block for firewood. Against the walls of the house and in the porch were piled mounds of hailstones. Every glasshouse in the village was a shattered ruin, vineries were destroyed, the grapes cut to pieces, and the vine branches hacked as with an axe. At Palmers Green hailstones fell that would not go into a tumbler, cattle were killed in the fields as by a rain of bullets; it was years before the effect of the storm was obliterated. Though it was the height of the summer the heaps of ice were unmelted even next day, the village looked as if it had been bombarded, there were neither glaziers nor glass to be found for repairs, and for nearly a week the Doctor's house remained with broken windows pasted over with brown paper. It was truly a never-to-be-forgotten hailstorm.

### 7.—THE CART ON THE GREEN.

In 1860 there arrived on the hill a large gypsy van. A well-to-do vehicle painted dark brown and drawn by a strong horse. It pitched on the green, which was then all open common ground, near the King's Head corner. The horse was led away to the stable, not turned loose on the grass to move on next day, and the whole arrival had an air of permanency. There was a door in the side from which steps descended. A window with lace curtains gave an appearance of refinement, and there were barge-boards of fancy woodwork under the eaves of the roof, a large portion of which was skylight. Neither the door nor the window was central, and it appeared that the interior was divided into an outer chamber, to which the steps gave access, and an inner apartment absolutely unlighted. There was no glittering brass stove, and there were no sleeping bunks, as in the basket woman's waggon, or the van of the dark skinned folk, who from time to time camped in Jew's Corner Lane and made clothes pegs, but next day frames of dull-coloured portraits were placed on each side of the doorway, a name board and price lists were added, and behold the van was a Photographic Establishment. It was entirely a new sensation in the village, and caused considerable excitement. It remained for some weeks on the green, and the admiring public came to be " taken." The portraits were all glass positives, but were, however, a considerable advance on the earlier Daguerreotypes both as regards artistic merit and popular prices. The taking of the likeness was a serious and lengthy performance, and the exposures lasted fully half a minute; no wonder the prolonged effort to look pleasant produced either a furious scowl or a fixed grin. Winifred was dressed in her best black silk frock, with a saucer neck and short puffed sleeves, and her coral necklace, and went with the Doctor himself to be photographed. She was given a rose to hold in her hand, and solemnly gazed into the camera for what seemed an unending space of time, rigidly endeavouring to hold her breath and not move a muscle till the cap was safely back upon the lens. Then the photographer departed into his inner chamber. There were mysterious sounds of running water, washings and splashings, combined with a strong aroma of ether which filled the air and gave her a light-headed sensation. Presently the man returned with a dripping plate, backed with black paint, on which was her

# WINCHMORE HILL.

portrait in various shades of greenish grey. It was pronounced a success, and she again underwent the ordeal in another position. Each picture was unique in those days and good or bad rested on its own merits. The next day the photographs were fetched home, finished and perfect, each in an oval frame with four gilt corners, surrounded by a piping of crimson velvet, and a square outer case of brownish purple leather paper. Two years later a photographer came to the village and produced cartes-de-visite, which were an immense improvement on the old method, and there were probably many people besides Winifred who thought that you obtained a *carte de visite* by a *visit* to the *cart* on the green.

## 8.—ESPRIT DE CORPS.

In the early sixties began what is known as the Volunteer movement, and in Tottenham a corps was formed called the 33rd Middlesex Rifle Volunteers.

The Doctor and his brother-in-law were among the earliest recruits. They attended the drills and firing practice by taking the Red Omnibus to Tottenham, or by walking the five miles each way. The men and officers of the corps worked like navvies to build their huge butt in the Lea Marshes; it was formed by raising a considerable earthwork crowned by a mass of faggots, and the Doctor entered into the new movement with much enthusiasm. At first he was very diffident about the opinions of his patients, there being so many Quakers in the village who regarded all forms of soldiering as wicked, and opposed the idea of Volunteer corps in every way. When Winifred had seen her father in all the glory of his new uniform, she chattered about it to an acquaintance, and in consequence received one of the sharpest scoldings in her experience for gossiping about his affairs, and not minding her own business—she being at the time about seven and her friend having reached the mature age of five; but in spite of the rebuff she shared the Doctor's excitement when he narrated how many bull's-eyes he had made, and he painted her a real target to shoot at with her bow and arrows. It was made of thick mill board, and a piece of gold paper was obtained from London to make the bull's-eye. She had also a set of little flags, red, green, and white, such as the marker used at the butt, and ran decorations of scarlet braid on an old grey jacket to wear in the back garden, and later her best dress was adorned with Austrian knots on the sleeves in imitation of her father's uniform. The Volunteers were so various in height, in the beginning of things, that they were known as " Her Majesty's Mixed Pins," and one gentleman of this corps was portrayed in a picture in " Punch " because he was obliged to stand upon a felled tree in order to reach to load his rifle. The men were armed with the old muzzle loading Long Enfield, weighing about 10 lbs. Winifred could hardly lift the Doctor's rifle, but learned her drill from him with a little old rusty fowling piece. He remained always a private, though he was pressed to accept a commission more than once; he felt his professional duties were so likely to interfere with his regimental ones, and would not undertake what he could not perform. The original uniform was a grey cloth tunic and trousers, trimmed with narrow red braid, peaked cap with a plume of black and scarlet horse hair, tan leather cross belts, pouches, etc., afterwards the plume was changed for a small woolly pom-pom; each man had also a linen haversack and a padded leather knee cap, like a horse's, to use when kneeling to fire. The Doctor was one of the crack shots of his corps, and twice the picked man for Wimbledon. He brought home a good field glass as a prize, and also a bunch of purple bell heather,

## WINCHMORE HILL.

and Tonbridge Well's heath with its waxen blossoms, some cotton grass, and a damp paper packet of sundews. These were a great excitement as none of them grew near Winchmore Hill.

Little people were taken more seriously in those days than they seem to be now. When Winifred was five years old Ann Pratt's Botany was first published in shilling monthly numbers; a specimen was brought to the house, and her father called her into the Study to ask whether she would like him to take the book in for her. She was delighted, and as the work was not completed for about three years she gradually learnt to know numbers of plants from the illustrations, which she only met with on her rambles in other counties many years later. She had not many new books of her own, and " Ann Pratt " became a valued friend and was always known as The Botany Book par excellence. The Doctor remained in the 33rd Middlesex till the terrible hiatus occurred in 1869, when the omnibuses were taken off the road, and the railway not yet open for traffic. The Tottenham 'bus was the first to go, and with the increasing population, his practice did not allow time for eight or ten miles walking whenever he attended firing practice or drill. When the 33rd was formed the word Corps was not so familiar as it is now, and Dicky P. once told the Doctor that his father was not at home because he was dining with his Corpse.

### 9.—THE VELOCIPEDE.

There was a great excitement in Hoppers Road one evening in the early sixties, when Mr Charles S. appeared riding down the hill on his new Velocipede. The natives called it a Philosopher, that being the nearest they could get to the word. It was a cumbrous vehicle upon four wooden wheels, and must have been most fatiguing to push along the moment the gradient was against it. When the Doctor had looked it over and examined its mechanism carefully he shook his head and said, " It was all very well for people to try and make self-propelled vehicles, but they were never likely to succeed, because while a man was moving a carriage in which he was seated he must always incur the fatigue of carrying his own weight plus that of the machine, and that could never be borne for any length of time or with much rapidity of motion." He lived to ride freely on tricycles, and to see the land full of ubiquitous wheels. When the old high " ordinary " was first introduced, boys used to call out, " Is that all that is left of your trap?" as it appeared to be reduced to one wheel only. The first tricycle the Doctor purchased weighed about 120 lbs., and carried two riders back to back, and, in his case, a white Pomeranian dog, who found plenty of room between the two; the pedals were on long levers with direct action, and the leg motion extraordinary. The driving wheel was five feet in diameter and was on one side, while there were two very small wheels on the other. The rims were extremely narrow, and the solid rubber tyres were cemented in, and were continually becoming partly or wholly detached. The seat was a large flat platform of metal and had a blue cloth cushion like a carriage seat mattressed with *hard buttons,* which was fastened on by a leather strap and buckle. The steering was effected by a long lever acting on the foremost of the little side wheels, a mere touch taking vast effect. Perhaps the most primitive portion of the whole machine was the brake, which was simply a bar of iron, raised and lowered by means of a chain, which dragged on the ground and checked the pace of the tricycle by digging its end into the gravel. Notwithstanding its many shortcomings, when viewed from a modern standpoint, it was very fast, and when two passengers were on board the fatigue of riding was comparatively small. Some years later a *very light* lady's tricycle was purchased, chiefly for Winifred's benefit, not weighing more than 80 lbs., but this was in the eighties and belongs to modern history.

### 10.—OLD-FASHIONED TOY DOGS.

The Green Dragon had the character of being always a sporting house. It was a low white building with a fiery specimen of what our forefathers called a " loathly worm " on the sign above its eaves. There was a pillared portico, the top of which was a gay garden of scarlet geraniums and gold calceolarias. Fine trees shaded the roadway on either side, and on summer evenings and Sunday afternoons the gravelled yard was filled with vehicles of all sorts—waggonettes, char-a-bancs, dogcarts, smart gigs, and American trotting cars. In earlier days it had been a great place for cock fights, and many a prize fight had the " Fancy " held there in by-gone times; but all that was changed, and its glory had departed. It was usually very quiet in the earlier part of the day; a few labourers went there for their eleven o'clock or four o'clock, and there was necessarily bustle and fuss at the times of departure and return of the omnibuses. In the later sixties the landlord of the Green Dragon was William Macdonald, the well-known dog fancier. He was indeed one of the fathers of the Toy Dog Fancy. He was a big Scotsman with a remarkably fine beard, and was constantly to be seen driving in a diminutive trotting car with a leg on each shaft, between which was a rat of a pony, a dark brown beastie, clean limbed and fine drawn as a little race horse. It travelled with a running action at a wonderful speed, and was said to be able to do twenty miles within the hour. Old " Mac " wore a large Tam o' Shanter, a short dark coat, and shepherd's plaid waistcoat, and continuations, and as he drove his great red brown beard parted in the middle and blew outwards over his shoulders. His toy dogs were at that time of very high value. The tiny bull terrier, Daisy, who had won over £100 in prizes, was so square and cobby, she would put to shame the weeds that go by the name of toy bull terriers in these days. Duke and Molly, the Italian greyhounds, were higher in quality than almost anything that has been seen since. The pugs had much longer noses than at present and their ears were trimmed off close to their heads. One of them, named Charley, after winning many prizes, was sold to the Marquis of Huntly for £40, a price which in those days created a greater sensation than ten times the amount would do now. There were also diminutive black and tan terriers, and silky white Maltese. All these were kept in the bar-parlour under Miss Macdonald's care, but in the stabling and kennels outside were fine specimens of many more breeds. Rella, the winning white bull terrier, was a very different type to the show bitches of the present day. Her weight was barely 16 lbs., and she would pass as a somewhat short-faced " White English " now-a-days. There were red and brindled dogs like her, and some large pugs were also kennelled outside. In the meadow at a respectable distance from the house dwelt a tame fox, with a wire run, and a barrel for his kennel. In those days dog shows were few and far between, and the all-governing Kennel Club was not yet in existence. Mr Macdonald was always willing to show his favourites, and anyone who knew him must recall him with a kindly memory, whenever they think of the " Green Dragon."

## 11.—CHINA ASTERS.

There was a tradition that the parishes of Edmonton and Enfield had the privilege of free standing in Covent Garden Market, because they supplied London with vegetables during the great Plague. Whether there was anything in the statement or not, they are now and always have been, a land of market gardens and nurseries. There were greenhouses beyond the " King's Head," which were managed by a Scotsman, whose pelargoniums in summer and Chinese primroses and cinerarias in winter and early spring were of great renown both in the village and London town. He was a kind man who would always find a plant for a penny to be the glory of a small person's garden. There were other nurseries within a mile of the hill, and once upon a time Winifred and the Boy decided to buy pots of China Asters as a birthday present for the Mother. First they tramped down Ford's Grove, where the trees made a tunnel of greenery and the tall hedgerows arched over the road side ditches, and wide grass tracts edged the road, and on by the shadeless Hyde footpath to the cottage beyond, where the market garden was gay with long beds of asters, white, pink, and purple, but they found none to be sold in pots. Back they came through the Hyde and followed the narrow windings of Firs Lane. The ditches on each side were very deep and had a tragic interest, as once the wheels of a thrashing machine that was being dragged from one farm to another had broken down the rotten bank, and the unwieldy mass had overbalanced into the ditch, crushing to death one of the men who was with it. The children found the road long and dusty, past the Moat Pond and Widow Andrews's lonely black cottage where the road turns towards Highfield Row, past the end of the Barrowell Green Lane, and the large house of Firs Farm, till they reached a nursery garden beyond. Here hope revived, and though they were leg weary, rejoicing filled their hearts, for they found what they sought in perfection. But it was so difficult to choose. There was an *embarras de richesse*. Would the Mother like a deep purple and a pure white, a crimson, a pale pink, or that delicate lilac? It was so impossible to choose that

*Old Cottages on Church Hill near the King's Head.*

in the end they bought them all. The Boy was very small. His arms could hardly embrace two flower pots, and Winifred was terribly burdened with three. Surely it would be better to wait at the corner by Huxley Farm for the dinner-time 'bus. They were hungry, and they were tired. It seemed as if that 'bus would never come. At last there was a sound of wheels. It proved to be only the flour cart, which had been to the Mill, with Tom Bury's old mare in the shafts, who was a chestnut, marked over her quarters with white, exactly as if a sack of flour had been emptied over her back. However, all things are said to come to him who will but wait, and at last the omnibus rattled up to the corner between the hay ricks and the forget-me-not pond, and rather resentfully pulled up at the children's call. It was nearly empty, and horses and men alike were hurrying home to their mid-day meal. "What would you charge to let us ride home?" asked Winifred. "Sixpence each," answered the conductor. The children's faces fell. They had not so much left, and in any case dared not run into such reckless extravagance. "Couldn't you take us for threepence?" they said. "What! with all them flower pots?" was the scornful rejoinder. The whip cracked, the horses strained at their traces, and away went the coach in a cloud of dust. It was past one o'clock when the lumbering vehicle passed the Doctor's house, and his wife was at the gate wondering where her children had gone, and it was at least half-an-hour later when, dusty and starving and utterly worn out, Winifred and the Boy arrived at home, still gallantly clutching the five flower pots of china asters, the white and the pink, and the purple, the crimson and the delicate mauve, and how the Mother valued her birthday present none but a mother could know.

## 12.—CAKES, ETC.

If an unexpected visitor turned up by the mid-day omnibus, he came, of course, to dinner and to tea. It was an old-fashioned maxim that an invitation to the most important meal of the day included the evening meal also, and nothing was considered more impolite than to hurry away early in the afternoon. If you had anyone to tea it was needful to buy a cake, and to do that meant a visit to Mrs Binsted's shop in Middle Lane. On the north side of the pond on the green was a pathway known as the "Trap Gates," or sometimes as the "Clappers." This led between hedges and fields to Vicars Moor Lane, which, like Compton Lane, connected the village with the main road a quarter of a mile to the east of it, and Middle Lane lay between the other two. First there was a high, quickset hedge, then a few cottages standing back in long gardens where cabbages and potatoes received more attention than floriculture, and at the end of the row the shop of Mr and Mrs Binsted, Bakers and Confectioners. There were sixpenny cakes, and shilling cakes, such as are now called Madeira, and they were kept till wanted on a high shelf in a tin labelled Pound Cake. There were other things there also far more interesting than confectionery. To begin with the shop stood back from a front garden always gay with flowers. On a high rockery was a collection of ferns that could be found nowhere else but in Ann Pratt's Botany. Plenty of bracken and male fern might be picked in the wood or lanes, but here were harts-tongues and prickly ferns, parsley ferns, and many others. In the middle of the garden was a little pond full of goldfish, and in the centre of the pond was a real fountain, which played when Mrs Binsted was persuaded to turn on the tap. On the counter in the shop, among the sweet-smelling loaves of in the end they bought them all. The Boy was very small. His arms could hardly embrace two flower pots, and Winifred was terribly burdened with three. Surely it would be better to wait at the corner by Huxley Farm for the dinner-time 'bus. They were hungry, and they were tired. It seemed as if that 'bus would never come. At last there was a sound of wheels. It proved to be only the flour cart, which had been to the Mill, with Tom Bury's old mare in the shafts, who was a chestnut, marked over her quarters with white, exactly as if a sack of flour had been emptied over her back. However, all things are said to come to him who will but wait, and at last the omnibus rattled up to the corner between the hay ricks and the forget-me-not pond, and rather resentfully pulled up at the children's call. It was nearly empty, and horses and men alike were hurrying home to their mid-day meal. " What would you charge to let us ride home?" asked Winifred. " Sixpence each," answered the conductor. The children's faces fell. They had not so much left, and in any case dared not run into such reckless extravagance. " Couldn't you take us for threepence?" they said. " What ! with all them flower pots?" was the scornful rejoinder. The whip cracked, the horses strained at their traces, and away went the coach in a cloud of dust. It was past one o'clock when the lumbering vehicle passed the Doctor's house, and his wife was at the gate wondering where her children had gone, and it was at least half-an-hour later when, dusty and starving and utterly worn out, Winifred and the Boy arrived at home, still gallantly clutching the five flower pots of china asters, the white and the pink, and the purple, the crimson and the delicate mauve, and how the Mother valued her birthday present none but a mother could know.

## 12.—CAKES, Etc.

If an unexpected visitor turned up by the mid-day omnibus, he came, of course, to dinner and to tea. It was an old-fashioned maxim that an invitation to the most important meal of the day included the evening meal also, and nothing was considered more impolite than to hurry away early in the afternoon. If you had anyone to tea it was needful to buy a cake, and to do that meant a visit to Mrs Binsted's shop in Middle Lane. On the north side of the pond on the green was a pathway known as the " Trap Gates," or sometimes as the " Clappers." This led between hedges and fields to Vicars Moor Lane, which, like Compton Lane, connected the village with the main road a quarter of a mile to the east of it, and Middle Lane lay between the other two. First there was a high, quickset hedge, then a few cottages standing back in long gardens where cabbages and potatoes received more attention than floriculture, and at the end of the row the shop of Mr and Mrs Binsted, Bakers and Confectioners. There were sixpenny cakes, and shilling cakes, such as are now called Madeira, and they were kept till wanted on a high shelf in a tin labelled Pound Cake. There were other things there also far more interesting than confectionery. To begin with the shop stood back from a front garden always gay with flowers. On a high rockery was a collection of ferns that could be found nowhere else but in Ann Pratt's Botany. Plenty of bracken and male fern might be picked in the wood or lanes, but here were harts-tongues and prickly ferns, parsley ferns, and many others. In the middle of the garden was a little pond full of goldfish, and in the centre of the pond was a real fountain, which played when Mrs Binsted was persuaded to turn on the tap. On the counter in the shop, among the sweet-smelling loaves of

*Middle Lane, looking West. The St. Paul's Church Institute stands on the site of the Old Wooden Stable.*

new bread, stood a squirrel's cage with a wheel, which he spun rapidly with much apparent enjoyment. His performance was reported to resemble that of the donkey in Carisbrooke Castle. In the window, among the bottles of barley sugar and rose lozenges hung cages of canaries and linnets. On the shelf above the great bins of bran, barley, and pollard, were cages of white mice, and piebald rats, and guinea pigs; and rabbits of all sorts of colours had their hutches in the barn outside. "Moses," the old brown owl, sat blinking among the rafters; conceited game bantams strutted about the yard and crowed saucily at the spangled Hambros and ordinary barn-door fowls. When Mrs Binsted called from her shop door, pigeons came from all around, and they even perched upon her shoulders. There were pouters and tumblers, iridescent blue rocks, and, more lovely than all, pure white fantails, and with them sweet-voiced ring-doves, such as are usually kept in cages. It took a long time to buy a cake from Mrs Binsted! There was also a dog, a large brindled greyhound, which had a bad name in the village as a notorious thief. "Give a dog a bad name and hang him" is a true saying, and he was certainly once innocent of a crime laid to his charge. The Doctor's wife made a black currant pudding. There was no larder in her house, only a cold cupboard under the front door steps, and a perforated meat safe hung high upon the wall of the back kitchen. After its first appearance the remains of the pudding were put into this safe, and next day, when they were to be warmed up for dinner, the housewife found to her horror that only the cold suet crust remained—all the fruit had disappeared. The surgery boy was washing physic bottles at the sink, making a vast rattling of small shot to clean the pale green glass. His mistress noticed the tell-tale blackness of the currant juice at the corners of his mouth. "William, do you know anything about this pudding?" she enquired. "I expect," replied the culprit stolidly, "it was all stole by Binsted's dawg." There was another shop in Middle Lane where children were always made welcome. It adjoined the "Queen's Head." There were in the window bottles of sweets with mottoes, "Kiss me quick," "Love me," etc., acid drops, clove balls, brandy balls, and long sugar sticks striped like barbers' poles, which paid toll to all small customers. At Christmas time they received presents of bunches of candles, miniature tallow dips, scarlet, yellow, blue, and emerald green; but these last Winifred was never allowed to handle for fear of the arsenic with which they were coloured. The dear old folk at that shop must be for ever remembered for their kindness. Their name was Waters, and their personality so marked that in the language of the district Middle Lane was universally spoken of as "Waterses" Lane.

The Ford Filcaps Farm

## CHAPTER IV.

### BIRDS' NESTS.

The children of the old village knew nothing of the duty of "making Nature notes," or of "taking an intelligent interest in the wild life around them," but they were taught the old story of "Eyes and No Eyes," and would have been ashamed not to know the trees and flowers, birds, nests, and eggs, the common butterflies and moths, and the fishes in the New River. While they were almost babies the Mother taught them how to recognise trees in Winter by the bark, and in Spring she showed them the crimson jewel on the filbert bush in the corner of the garden, which was the female bloom, and explained that the tasselled catkins grew no nuts. She introduced them to the little doves in the columbine blossom, and the ship's keel in the sweet pea, and spread the butterfly wings also that gave the reason for the long Latin name to the tribe of peas, beans, and vetches. They sowed mustard and cress in the letters of their own names, and learnt how one seed differed from another, and the Doctor helped them to find birds' nests. In the quickset hedge in Compton Lane was a hedge sparrow's nest, all soft green moss and twigs, lined with the hair of a red cow. The four eggs were as blue as the turquoise in the Mother's old enamelled necklace. In nearly every holly bush they found a blackbird's or a thrush's nest. Outside they were very much alike, being built of moss and rootlets, but within the blackbird finishes hers softly with moss while the song-thrush plasters her house with cow dung. The thrush's egg was more sky blue than the hedge sparrow's, and was spotted thickly at one end with deepest purple. That of the blackbird was green and flecked all over with light tan colour. "If you take a robin's nest you are sure to break your leg," and the robins seemed to know they were safe, and took very little trouble to conceal their nursery. There was a nest in the bank by the field gate—a loose mass of feathers and grass lined with down and horsehair, which contained five pearly white eggs spotted with red. Another robin's nest was in a wonderful place. You might pass it fifty times, because you would never look at the rusty old beer warmer, a conical "tooty tooty" with a curling ear, lying among the rubbish in the Park shrubbery beyond the tarred fence. That piece of ground behind the houses was a perfect museum of old kettles and saucepans, broken china and earthenware, and among the tall fool's parsley lay the beer warmer, and in it a robin's nest, and among the delicate pale coloured eggs was one large greenish brown one, twice the size of the others but not so large as a thrush's or blackbird's. It was a cuckoo's egg. They usually lay their eggs in hedge sparrows' nests, so this was rather out of the common, and it was difficult to imagine how the big bird could have laid it in the narrow iron pot, unless, as has been asserted, she placed it there with her beak. There used to be stories of hen cuckoos having been seen flying over the orchards carrying an egg in their bills, searching for a nest in which to place it, and it appeared as if it could not have been laid among the robin's eggs in the beer warmer in any other way. The Doctor hoped to see the birds hatched, but, unfortunately, the nest was stolen and lost. The cooking utensil in question was about six inches wide at the mouth and ten or eleven in depth at the apex of the cone. It was lying on its side with the nest at right angles to the orifice. In the Doctor's garden redstarts were very common; locally they were known as firetails, from the bright orange feathers under the tail. They built year after year in the same crack

## WINCHMORE HILL.

of the garden wall, the nest of dry grass and moss, and the eggs the pale blue of a forget-me-not blossom. The misselthrushes nested high up the fork of a lime tree. Like the song-thrush, the nest was lined with mud, but an inner finishing of soft grass was added. The eggs were large and very handsome, being grey blue, spotted and blotched with red brown and brownish purple almost black. There was something wild and weird about this large bird who sang his loudest when a thunderstorm was raging and rain pouring in deluges. He is called the storm-cock, and appears to exult in bad weather and rejoice in riot and desolation. If one could see into his mind we should probably find his song was a Te Deum about juicy snails, fat slugs, and worms of earth. At the edge of the wood behind the dressmaker's cottage some sparrows built a nest woven of odds and ends of silk, wool, cotton, and thread ends of all colours, feathers, hairpins, and scraps of wire. It was more a rag bag than a nest, and the ladies of the village might have identified fragments of their Sunday frocks. The house sparrow does not hold with any act of uniformity. It builds with any material at hand, and lays eggs varying in the same nest from pink and white to grey and olive green. At the other end of the wood was a steep bank above a dry ditch nearly full of dead oak leaves. Half-way up the slope was a hollow place, the mouth of a rabbits' burrow that had fallen in, and there the oak leaves appeared to have rolled themselves into a compact ball. On closer inspection an opening was visible at one side; the mass of leaves was a nightingale's nest. It was bound together with grass bents and lined with softer grass and rootlets, and contained four dull olive-green eggs, scarcely differing in colour from the material of which it was composed. The wood was full of nightingales in the early Summer, and no doubt there were many nests, but there were only three of these discovered, the concealment of colour and position was so complete; two nests were found in the wood, and the third in the bank of a roadside ditch at a point nearly opposite to the present gates of the Great Northern Fever Hospital. There were jays' nests high in the spruces, and wood pigeons built in the larch plantations. The pheasants were few and far between, but the eggs were seen occasionally if the children were among the young birch saplings picking wood anemones, and waterfowl nested all round the lake in Groveland's Park and on the islands. They were so protected they scarcely counted as wild birds. The prettiest nests of all were the chaffinches. More than an inch thick of moss and lichen lined with the softest feathers, and with brown eggs and darker zig-zag markings that looked as if you could read the words if you knew the language. The colouring always suggested Mocha stones. The greatest contrast to the chaffinch's nest was that of the lesser whitethroat or hay-tit, who builds a transparent structure which is a mere network of grass bents; it is in reality very strongly put together, but always looks unfinished and too frail to support the pale spotted eggs within. There was a willow wren's house in a hole in the dairyman's haystack, with fourteen tiny white eggs deeply spotted with pink, and her namesake, Jenny Wren, built a domed dwelling of leaves and moss against the red trunk of a yew tree inside the Highfield Park wall, halfway down Compton Lane. It faced due south, and was almost invisible, although there was no attempt at concealment; it relied on colour alone to escape the eye of the marauder. The eggs were like those of the willow wren, but very much paler, indeed so faintly spotted as to be almost white. There were always young owlets in the breeding season in a hollow oak in Highfield Park. They were white barn owls, like the one in the old story which Pat shot when he was crossing a churchyard in the gloaming. It lay among the tombstones with outspread wings, and he rushed home pale with terror because "begorra he had shot one of the blessed Cherubim." The children loved to see the white owls flitting silently among the oak trees in the summer twilight. Highfield Park was for many years their free playground. There were two large meadows, known as the upper ten-acre and the lower ten-acre, separated by a fence of iron hurdles. A gravel footpath ran all round the small estate, with a wide belt of bushes and fine trees known as the Shrubbery, which was divided from the pathway by a dwarf quickset hedge. The children had a geography of their own and called the great oaks by names. Two of the largest were Broken Bough and Splinter—the latter had been split by lightning— and beyond were the Oak apple tree and the Owl tree, which was massed with dark ivy, the stem of which was as thick as a man's thigh. The soft " whoo-whoo " of the white owls and the hissing of the baby owls in the nest, the rustling of small things in the grass, the grunt of a hedgehog, the nibbling of the sheep and baaing of lambs in the upper ten-acre, the stamp of a horse's hoof as he shook off the gnats by the pond, the white mist wreaths rising from the grass and hiding the trunks of the trees so that their tops appeared to float on a silver sea. Who could wish to go home and exchange all this for a closely shut up room and quiet evening amusements by the light of a Moderator lamp? But what must be must be, and it was too late to stay out longer. Soon after they had returned home one evening the Doctor's brother-in-law came in looking white and scared. He had been an evening walk since his return from the City by the six o'clock 'bus. He hurried the Doctor into the front garden to listen to the screams of a woman that he was sure was being murdered. The cries were terrible. He felt as if his blood was freezing in his veins. When they went outside not a sound was to be heard. There was a red afterglow in the

West. The young moon with the old one in her lap hung in the pale green sky above. The wood stretched like a black forest against the evening light. The world was very still. All was quiet in the village. The distant note of a corncrake scarcely broke the silence. There was a neigh from an old horse in the carrier's stable, the whirr of a passing cockchafer, and then suddenly from the edge of the wood came a ghastly cry. The sound was greeted by the Doctor's hearty laugh. "Why, man," he cried, "that is nothing but a screech owl."

Back of Highfield Row.

## CHAPTER V.

### REMINISCENCES.

"Some children," said the Doctor's wife, "are brought up, and some are lugged up;" but it is doubtful whether her own did not bring themselves up. When Winifred was between three and four years old she longed with all her little heart to be a boy. To tell the truth she was always hearing of the superiority of the "Lords of Creation," and felt that her importance would gain immensely by the metamorphosis, and being an egotistical little person she longed greatly to better herself if it could be done. She confided her ambition to the ever-sympathetic ear of her grandmother, who, kind old lady, sagely remarked—"Well! we must see what the new Parliament can do. They are going to do *everything*; so we must wait and see." To Winifred the laughing remark had the value of a prophecy. All her hopes, as so many other people's have done before and since, were centred in the election of the new Parliament.

At length the great day came. The Doctor, after some grumbling because those who "chose to undertake the governing of the country would not do it without bothering him," duly recorded his vote for "the gentlemen's candidate," and Winifred waited and hoped. It was too serious and important a matter to be talked about; but, like the parrot, she "thought the more," and few grown-ups can have any idea of the tragedy of disappointment when she found it had been "all a take in," and that she was condemned to wear her hated petticoats all her life, and would always be expected to "love her needle" and "sit still like a lady." The petticoat grievance was a reasonable one, as the Doctor and his wife were old-fashioned people and kept Winifred in skirts below her ankles, while those of other little girls of her age were up to their knees. When she grew big enough to climb trees and take long walks alone she spent many an hour endeavouring to make invisible darns in those skirts. Thorns and tenterhooks appeared to have a spite against her, and however careful she tried to be, she seemed to get more muddy and ragged than anyone could have believed possible. It is the ambition of every woman to have a house of her own, but Winifred's beginnings were decidedly troglodytic; when she was a tiny child, it was her great delight to make the Doctor dig a large hole in the garden, in which she could sit. His energies usually gave out when the cavity was some two feet square and perhaps eighteen inches deep; and, indeed, she was rather alarmed when that great depth was attained, lest if he put his spade in much further he should fall through into Australia, where everyone lived head downwards. At that time she was a lonely little maid with no one to play with, and had to be happy alone and amuse herself. A turned-down flower pot served as a seat, and she collected toads from under the leaves of the Winter heliotrope, black and yellow newts—effets, as they are called in North Middlesex—out of the coal cellar, and frogs from the area, and kept them in her hole, which was too deep for them to jump out of.

One hot Sunday morning a painful tragedy occurred. She had just found a fine young frog under the leaves of the Chinese day-lily, when she was called to get ready for Church. To keep him safe she covered him with a small disused hand-light. He was left in the shade, but, alas! the sun neared the zenith, the shadows shortened,

80 degrees in the shade was nearer 120 degrees in the sun, and when she returned home poor froggie was as dead as a door nail. All his limbs were extended, and his corpse stood stiffly up against the glass as rigid and hard as if he were made of bronze. Poor Froggie would never go wooing any more, and little Winifred felt herself a murderer, and despair entered into her soul. She cried bitterly about that unfortunate frog, and wondered what it would be like to be roasted alive in hell. The sermons she had to listen to on Sundays contained much matter about worms and flames, and being conscious that she was always such a naughty little girl, however hard she tried to be good, she never doubted that if she died she would go to the hot place. She had a rooted belief in Old Nick as portrayed in the "Ingoldsby Legends," which the Doctor read to her before bed-time, as she sat on his lap in the rocking chair, till she nearly knew them by heart. At one time her mind was occupied by ideas of buried treasure. In stories beginning "Once upon a time" great wealth was found in most surprising ways, but she was convinced such things only occurred in books, and, like giants and fairies, would never come her way; but she might bury something of which she alone would know the secret—only what could it be? At this time the Mother set the " screwdrawer " (escritoire) to rights, and among other things turned out a sample box of old pens. No other family would have put all the used pens back into a box and kept them ten years or so; but there they were, at least fifty samples, gold pens, silver pens, bronze pens, and black pens, pens like hands with the index figure for the nibs, short nibs, long nibs, points turned up and points turned down, an extraordinary collection of varieties, and they were all given to Winifred. She played with them for a few days, and then decided

they would do for treasure. With great solemnity she dug as deep a hole as she could make with a trowel, and planted the little tin box of pens under a black currant bush. But the extraordinary part of the matter was that, though she never forgot them, it was years before she dug them up again! What became of them after that I know not. Possibly their condition was such that little value was left even to " make believe " about.

When she was eight years old she became the proud possessor of a map, enlarged with the help of her uncle from the Ordnance Survey, of all the roads within one mile of home, and anywhere in that radius she might walk alone.

She could read by the time she was four, and was soon able to write well enough to send letters to the Mother when she was away at the seaside, not baby letters only, but ones containing the news of the house and village.

Winifred's world was a very small one, and she lacked imagination.

The fig tree against the garden wall, close to the crack where the redstarts built, was the one out of which Adam and Eve made aprons, and they pinned them together with the thorns from the gooseberry bushes. No doubt there was a connection with the saying, that " Mend well went to Heaven, rag-tag stayed upon earth, but the Devil ran away with pin together." Joseph was put into Vicarsmoor Well, and it was also on the brickwork edge of it that Rebecca sat and drew water for her sheep. It was the Ding Dong Bell Well into which poor pussy was put by little Jacky Thin, and from whose depth she was rescued by Johnny Stout.

The mouse in " Dickery, Dickery Dock " ran up the tall clock in the Doctor's study, and—

" Dickery, Dickery, dum tree,
The cat ran up the plum tree,"

referred to the great Reine-Claude greengage. The cock robins buried the Babes in Winchmore Hill Wood, where there were oak leaves enough to cover any number of corpses, and blackberries for them to eat before they lay down and died.

The " Round pond and a pretty pond too " was, of course, the one on the green, but the second line—

" About it wild daisies and violets grew "—

referred to some former time, as there were no violets there now.

" The tall weeping willows " that shaded it round were regarded as poetic licence: the willows were there, only they didn't weep; and so on in all the stories she read or heard told—her little world held them all, or else she gave them up as a bad job. Highfield Park was not then the free playground it became later, but in hay-time she was allowed to go there, if any of the women servants from the great house were at work; but she always slipped away to be petted by the men, and ride in the empty waggon or astride on Dobbin's back. There was a curious specimen of humanity often employed as oddman at Highfield. He was known as " Friday," or " Man Friday," and, as far as the Doctor could discover, had never possessed any other name. He was tall and gaunt and loose limbed, with long hair falling over his eyes in elf locks, and he was not quite " all there," but he was very kind to Winifred, who regarded him as a friend, and more than once she had sat in his lap while he lunched, and shared not only his bread and cheese but his beer.

She was friends with every dog in the village, even with Morgan's greyhounds. There was a pack of thirty or forty of these dogs, and they ran in a large field adjoining the Trapgates. Sometimes they would jump the high quickset hedges and alarm passers-by. They were also exercised in the roads, and did a good deal of damage. Many a small dog was worried, or even killed, by them, to say nothing of cats or poultry. In the early days they were neither led nor muzzled, unless positively savage and unmanageable.

Nearly opposite the Doctor's house was that of Eaton, the carrier. He had two horses, gingerbread chestnuts or duns, with long silver manes and tails. The carrier was an important and responsible person, and his horses were well fed and strong, and did the journey to London and back two or three times in the week. Their tails were relied on to make fishing lines. The carrier also kept Muscovy ducks, and these or the geese on the green provided quills for floats. The surgery furnished corks, the Doctor's shot-belt leads, the woodstack or a ground-ash supplied a rod, and a farthing hook could be bought at Miss Lowen's—even a bent pin could be made to do in an emergency. The New River was free fishing to all, and if one of the children nearly fell in and escaped by a scramble, it took care to be quite dry before returning home, so no awkward questions should be asked.

The old High road was narrow, with wide grass edges, crossed by little grips every few yards, and with deeper ditches at the sides. Steady horses were needed for the long night journeys in Winter, and in foggy weather it was difficult to keep to the road. The Doctor usually walked the ten miles each way whenever he visited the " old Lady in Threadneedle Street," and on one October night found himself overtaken by a thick fog. Opposite to the " Cock " at Bowes Farm there stood a pump by the roadside, on one of the wide grass margins that gave the London Road its name of Green Lanes. The handle of the pump was to the North and the spout to the South. The children had this fact impressed upon them, because on this particular night the Doctor did not know it. He had reached the end of Alderman Sidney's wall and crossed the Bounds Green Road, and was adrift,

*The Old "Retreat," which stood at the corner of the Hagfields Footpath and Old Green Dragon Lane, looking towards Old Park Farm.*

so to speak, in the open. Pym's Brook was filling the whole valley with a dense white mist, and the yellow smoke of the city was rolling down to meet it. Cold, weary, and cheerless, he stopped to light his pipe, and unthinkingly turned to shelter the flickering lucifer match, and, too late, realised that he had lost his direction and had no conception which was his way home. He wandered off the roadway on to the turf, feeling more confused at every moment, when suddenly, to his great relief, he stumbled against the pump and knew where he was, but for the life of him he could not remember whether the spout or the handle was towards Winchmore Hill. He had to chance it, and by good luck found himself on the rising ground of King's Arms Bridge, and the fog rapidly thinning showed him the lights in the cottages at the foot of Alderman's Hill and the low one-storey hovels of Malice Row, which were built, it is said, to spite an opposite neighbour.

Winifred soon became a useful child, who could do shopping in the vilage and be trusted to pay the week's bills for her mother or grandmother. She was such a responsible person in this way that her cousin, who came from a West of England watering-place, and had never in her life been out walking by herself, suffered for it. She was sent with a half-witted servantgirl to pay the butcher's book, and came back without having seen it was properly receipted. Poor child, she knew nothing whatever about such things, but the old Lady regarded her as culpably ignorant for nine years of age, as she had employed Winifred as her little messenger for years. By this time the boy with the fair curls was becoming a person to be reckoned with, and he and Winifred played together. As with all children toys had their season. In autumn clay lanterns were greatly in fashion. They were formed of thin slabs of the tenacious yellow clay, and were rather damp and cold to handle. A candle end in a clay socket and a piece of glass for the front made a lamp which lighted a garden path as well as the family tin one from the shop.

"Knucklebones" were as absorbing as many people find games of Patience. Winifred had a set of five, laboriously chipped out of some very superior Cannel coal found in the cellar, which she was convinced were equal to real Whitby jet. She sat on one end of the stable step and practised her game on the other, and in these kindergarten days I would strongly advise a course of Knucklebones to train both the hand and the eye of any child. One-ers, two-ers, three-ers, four-ers, bonce, spanners, and pigs-to-market, to say nothing of all the variations of which they are capable, make as good a game of skill for a solitary girl or boy as could be wished. The Doctor made a wonderful pair of scales out of cocoanut shells, polished till they were like mahogany, and was most talented in cutting Jacob's wells out of apples, making walnut shell baskets, date-stone cribbage pegs, and pearls from haddocks' eyes. Of course there were indoor toys, a splendid box of bricks, dissected maps, spillikins, and many others.

A much valued swing hung in the park shrubbery above the old saucepans and broken crockery. Hoops, good useful iron ones, were loved as if they were sentient beings. Fishing was with Winifred a passion, not because she met with great success, but she enjoyed the long solitary afternoons by the river when she was allowed to follow the gentle craft in the beautiful grounds of Beaulieu. There was a bend in the river under a great pine tree, which was far from the house, and one of the most peaceful places possible. Near it was an eighteenth century ruin and grotto with ponds and rockeries, which was a sort of dream country. The trees of Beaulieu were a fine botanical collection. Are they still there? There were enormous Cedars of Lebanon and a Maidenhair tree as tall as a good-sized oak, and numbers of specimens of rare shrubs and forest trees of every variety.

## WINCHMORE HILL.

In the sixties a Mr Adams took the grocer's shop at the Wood corner. He was rather a remarkable man, and a good entomologist. He was also very musical, and had a great ambition to possess a chamber organ. He set himself steadily to work to obtain money for its purchase by catching butterflies and moths for the collectors, and came to Winchmore Hill because it was such good ground for his pursuit. He reared caterpillars also, and would name any specimen taken to him, and his presence in the village was a great interest to the Doctor's children. It was a triumphant moment to take him a goat-moth caterpillar, all crimson and orange like a piece of Christmas beef, or an apple-green privet hawk-moth larva, with mauve stripes upon its sides. The Doctor knew all the commoner butterflies and a few of the moths, but the latter were so numerous, and many rare ones abounded in the neighbourhood which only an expert could name for certain. These were all taken to the Wood corner, and Mr Adams never spared trouble in answering the children's questions. He made over £100 by his hobby, and purchased the organ he so much longed for. In the hot summer of 1868 there were a most unusual number of butterflies and moths of all kinds, including a perfect visitation of humming bird sphinxes, and on many elm trees an exudation of sticky matter was crowded with wasps, bees, and hornets. A particularly large nest of the wood wasp was built in a tall rosemary bush in the Grandmother's garden. This species is not common. The great stagshorn beetles were very common, not only in the wood, but in the village itself, and cockchafers could be caught by the dozen by searching in the white blossoms of the guelder roses or shaking the old filbert tree in the corner of the Doctor's garden. At one time an evening walk through the wood was a sure way of finding glow-worms, a few imprisoned under a glass gave enough light to see the time by a watch.

The filbert tree was in an angle of the wall, and made a

sort of bower, which was known by the strange name of "Jellypump Cottage," but a far grander edifice was built when the boy was old enough to help, and he dignified it by the high-sounding appellation of "Crown Palace." The tarred fence formed the back, the chief support of the front was the post used for the clothes line (most people washed at home in those days), logs and boughs, old clothes props and remnants of carpet formed roof and walls, and some rough thatching was added of the straw from physic bottle crates. The dwelling boasted two rooms at least four feet square, and the whole structure was so picturesque the Doctor sketched it, unfortunately only in pencil, as the effects of colour were worthy of any artist's palette.

Winifred made a little pathway of tesselated pavement up to the door: Small round pieces chipped from the many coloured fragments of crockery in the shrubbery, laid in circles and diamonds, and grounded with portions of broken flower pot. They were all placed in a setting of clay, which, alas! dried and shrank, so that the carefully worked out design was quickly kicked aside and ruined. How she longed for real cement, that it might have lasted for hundreds of years like the Roman pavement pictured in her history book. But not only Crown Palace and its pavement are things of the past; the house and garden have vanished away in the depths of the railway cutting. Highfield Park is unrecognisable. The upper ten-acre and the lower ten-acre, the pond where they sailed the "Torch" (which had a copper bottom) and the "Waterwitch," and loaded them with wriggling black tadpoles as cargoes of slaves, are all gone. The hollow tree, which the Doctor set on fire in taking a wasps' nest, the old wall of the Back Lane (now Compton Lane) with Lawyer Compton's fireplace left in it, the banks of sweet violets, the thickets of acacia bushes, hawthorn, lilac, and laburnum, the wild gardens of Lords and Ladies with their handsome spotted leaves, the wilder-

## WINCHMORE HILL.

ness of fool's parsley and butcher's broom, " Holly Bower," " Yew Shelter," where are they all now? All are destroyed and have vanished. At the bottom of Compton Lane there was a little dell, and at one side of it a huge pollard elm that must have been there for many centuries. The ivy that mantled it had a trunk of enormous thickness, and formed a network round the aged tree. This was cut down many years ago— long before any building was contemplated, and it was a work of ruthless destruction, as the timber can have been of little value, though the giant elm was in full health and foliage, for its beauty alone, it was worthy of preservation, and its undoubted antiquity should have caused its life to be spared.

The only piece of the Park that has escaped the builder is the St. Bartholomew's recreation ground, but even that is sadly altered, though it remains grass-land.

The eight mile stone, just beyond, stood in a lonely stretch of road on the grass by a marshy pond. The five-barred gate close by led to a field where bluebells and lady-smocks flourished and mushrooms might be gathered. Opposite the mile stone is the lane to Barrow Well green. After passing over the New River Bridge there was a stretch of vegetable garden, and a most peculiar one-roomed dwelling, shaped like a tool shed, the front perpendicular and the roof sloping away behind. Its door and window reminded one of a chapel. This was called Hope Cottage. The gardener's name was Tom Jolly, and he lived there with his old wife, and sold fruit and vegetables.

The Doctor was asked to paint a picture in a young lady's album, and he chose a view of this abode, writing under it :—

" The Residence of Thomas Jolly, Esq."

" Oh, why should we be melancholy? Who live in Hope and always Jolly."

## CHAPTER VI.

## THE WOOD.

That forbidden pleasures are the sweetest is universally acknowledged. No doubt that was the reason that the private parts of Winchmore Hill Wood were the most attractive places in the world.

In the old days the public footpath was rough and sparsely gravelled, fenced only on the side which adjoined the keeper's cottage. The other side was open, and wild unspoilt woodland stretched away to the Hoppers Road meadows and Southgate Lane. It was a primeval forest of oak and beech, birch and holly; the undergrowth was in many places dense as a jungle, and in high summer the foot tracks were almost hidden in luxuriant bracken. There was a dark plantation of spruce and larch, a veritable fir forest planted long ago, and the children explored every corner of it and knew its highways and byeways as the city dweller knows his streets. It was a happy hunting ground in more senses than one, for they were often the hunted ones, and the Demon who guarded the Enchanted Forest was the hunter. He was an alarming and remorseless Ogre, clothed in velveteens, tall and gaunt, and forbidding, with piercing black eyes and a nose like an eagle's beak. He was believed to be armed with all the powers of the law, almost to the point of inflicting capital punishment. He carried a long gun, and had he chosen to shoot them no one would greatly have blamed him!

They ran before him like hares, they lay hidden in deep ditches, or fern-brakes, till he had passed by, scarcely daring to breathe. They practised the art of walking over dead twigs noiselessly, and when safely out of his dominions they

*The Footpath through the Wood near the Keeper's Cottage, looking East.*

## WINCHMORE HILL.

bragged of courage and daring, to which nobody gave credence.

It was an Enchanted Forest indeed, millions of miles from London, or even from the pond on the green; wild and remote and mysterious, bounded only by dinner time, tea time, or the short winter twilight.

The fir forest with its carpet of brown needles, and the red trunks and dark green boughs of the spruces, the light green larches with their pink blossoms and ragged brown cones; Rabbit-hole Ditch with its mossy banks, where a few primroses could be found when the larches were in bloom. What a wonderland they all were! The crab-apple tree at the further end of the ditch made a bower of pink and white blossom, against a background of the young growth of the birches and hornbeams. There were gardens of blue dog-violets, and wood anemones by the thousand.

There is a perfect beauty about the dim recesses of an old wood, that gives a feeling of solemn awe, near akin to that which pervades an ancient abbey.

In one place was an enormous oak with a tall straight trunk, a huge column, branchless for an unusual height from the ground. The spread of its boughs made a verdant roof, and only here and there was a fragment of blue sky visible. The great tree made a circular hall floored with velvet moss, and walled round with close growing brushwood. It would have been hard to find this natural ballroom if the dry bed of the water-course had not passed beside it. In another part of the wood was a giant beech, whose trunk, even in this hidden land, was carved with many a name or initial. The exposed roots made delightful seats and the ground lay bare and brown, scattered with last year's leaves. The beech stood alone among the firs of the plantation, whose columned aisles led away in deep shadows around.

Those who have heard the voices of the woods, and loved

their whisperings in childhood, will hear them calling for ever in the after years, calling them to wild places, to country sights and sounds, to the unspoilt corners of the land, where they can forget that crowds, and cities, and struggling suburbs, even exist. The Spirit of the Woods and the Spirit of the Hills know their own, and when they call, their own must go forth and do them homage. Some of the weirdest places in the wood were the pits of white sand half-full of water, inky black by contrast, and overhung by bracken dazzlingly green in the sunlight, massed round the trunks of dark holly bushes, a few of the fronds reaching an extraordinary height among the shining prickled leaves. In leafy June the woodbine wreathed the holmtrees with long streamers of creamy white flowers. The wild guelder rose grew in the more open spaces with snowy cymes of blossom in early summer, and coral red berries in the autumn, not so orange scarlet as those of the mountain ash. These both loved the fringe of the wood at the side of Southgate Lane, raising their gaudy heads above a thicket of luscious dewberries and blackberries. In August and September there were wild stretches of heather every shade of mauve and grey and purplish pink, and the pale blossoms of the little yellow cow-wheat—which some botanists tell us, marks the land as the forest primeval—were scattered everywhere.

At the edge of the firwood were pre-historic ant hills, three feet high, and covering many square yards of ground; the rush-grown cart road and every path near them were peopled with the black and red citizens in myriads.

The stumps of the oaks from the last year's felling made their summer shoots with enormous leaves, and the earlier growth was crowded with green and brown oak galls. The children laid them in saucers of water with rusty nails, in a vain endeavour to make ink. In summer and autumn the wood was gay with lichens and fungi of every sort and kind;

each fallen log bore shelves of turkey tails with surfaces of grey velvet and the jagged tops of the stumps bristled with white and black stagshorns. The golden peziza lay like the yolk of an egg among the dead leaves, and the scarlet amonita flamed on the edge of the fir forest. The Doctor once brought home some large puff-balls that had burst and shed their spores; he arranged them on the top of the wall that divided his garden from the next, and greatly provoked the wrath of his neighbour, who mistook them for a row of grinning skulls! These large puff balls can be fried in slices like suet pudding, but they are not common. The small white earth-balls were very plentiful in the wood, looking like eggs upon the ground, but when exploded their contents resemble those of a sweep's soot-bag. At the edge of the wood on the field side, where there was warmth from the southern sun, lay a narrow path, where numbers of great boletus grew, looking like unwholesome sponges, and in some places were crowds of tan coloured lactarius, that appeared to be made of saddle leather and when broken exuded milk. There were gay patches of rosy russulas and sulphur yellow agaricus. Toadstools everywhere, purple, black, grey, or olive green. One variety was lovely to look upon, but no one who had once smelt its odour, would ever wish to meet with it again. It was phallus impudicus, the stinkhorn. It had a cone-shaped cap, beautiful as carved ivory, a thick white stem rising from a hemisphere of olive green jelly, and when in perfection was surmounted by a greenish black fools-cap set jauntily on one side. The smell was a combination of a gas escape and neglected drains. It grew usually under the holly trees, though it may be found far from them.

When in the heart of the wood it was easy to realise that at one time there had been continuous forest land, covering the greater part of Middlesex; and to feel that, perhaps, for a thousand years this corner of England had remained unaltered.

There were rabbits, weasels, and stoats, and one or two pole-cats had been shot sufficiently recently for them to be seen stuffed and set up in glass cases, in cottages. Vipers were rare, grass snakes abounded, especially near water, and once or twice a blind worm or slow-worm was found. It looked as if it were made of pinkish terra-cotta, glittering with a glaze brighter than that of the finest porcelain. There was an uncanny pleasure in taking home the harmless reptile twisted as an armlet or as a living necklace. They will remain in rigid stiffness wherever they are placed and have no evil smell. The wood abounded with hedgehogs; in the twilight their soft grunting might be heard in the pauses of the nightingale's song. It was delightful to see an old mother hedgehog taking her two babies out slugging and worming in the grass rides. The youngsters' prickles are quite soft and weak; when disturbed they will take refuge in flight, while their mother rolls herself into a spiney ball that defies marauders. The speed at which these little beasts can travel is marvellous. When first you watch one of them it remains like a huge sea-egg betraying life only by a gentle breathing; slowly it uncurls, the pointed snout and beady eyes appear, then the uncanny black hands and feet are unpacked, and with a wriggle the beastie turns over, and cautiously lengthens itself out. At first it seems hardly to move at all, but in a few moments it waxes bolder, and slowly hurries to the roadside. You see it enter the grass, and by the time you have taken two strides to the spot, it has vanished as completely as if it had sunk into the ground. The Doctor's terrier was clever at finding hedgehogs, and when he sniffed at the ball of mystery and pricked his nose the particular tone in which he gave tongue was unmistakable. Some dogs open them with their feet and kill them, but very few will do it, and it is a good thing, as the small animal does much good and little harm. Tramps and gypsies eat them, but they are safe from most of the dangers that menace their unprotected neighbours.

In Summer the wood was alive with birds and beasts: you heard the soft coo of the pigeon or the harsh scream of the jay. There were songsters in great numbers and of many varieties, both native and migrant. But it was lovely in autumn when the beech leaves turned from green to golden yellow and then to copper, and the bracken became fiery red and deep orange, and after that, when the fern had withered and shrivelled, and the frost had painted the brambles purple and gamboge and vermilion, and the hollies were loaded with scarlet berries; then a great stillness settled on the woodland, the chill winds whispered of the glories of the past summer, and rustled the hope that again there should be mouse-ear time for the birches, and tasselled catkins for the hazels, but for the moment all was dead and quiet and still.

Then on some January night a moaning would wail through the red trunks of the spruces, the moonlight which gleamed white on the lichened oak boughs, veiled itself in clouds, and the darkness of death closed round the Wood World. There was a sound that was almost inaudible, a hissing of snow feathers in the air, and when the morning broke, and the skies cleared, and a blood red sun rose over the Essex hills, Lo! the wood had become fairyland! Every bramble was a wreath of ice flowers and each bush and tree glittered in a wedding garment. Who that had once seen it could ever forget it?

## CHAPTER VII.

### THE HIVING OF THE BEES.

Under the eaves of the stable were a long row of straw bee hives, old-fashioned skeps, dome-shaped and buxom, and ranging in colour from bistre to ochre. There was nothing new-fangled or modern. The stable was storage for the stack of birch faggots and oak logs, which were used for firewood. The chopping block and hatchet, the garden tools, and the wheelbarrow, were kept there, and the manger was the authorised receptacle for blacking bottles and brushes, dirty boots, oil and bathbrick. The only thoroughfare to the back door was through it, and on the whitewashed wall some errand boy had scored up in lead pencil the scornful rhyme—

" Oh, Salts and Senna don't ye grieve for me,
    I'd rather go to Alabama than a Doctor's Squash I'd
    be "—

a gibe levelled at the factotum, aged twelve, who wandered slowly at his own time, round the village with the medicine basket. Birch faggots have many uses, and the arrival of a new load had its tragic, not to say pathetic, side. The stumpy remains of the old birch rod were taken down from above the picture of lilies and roses in the dining-room and consigned to the flames, and a graceful long-tailed new edition of the Word-of-Command took its place. Tickle Toby was firmly bound together by the Doctor himself, and, though seldom used, its presence was decidedly awe inspiring. To take it down was equivalent to the reading of the Riot Act, a proceeding which is well known often to quench

## WINCHMORE HILL. 69

disturbances without the necessity of resorting to ball cartridge.

At the same time a freshly piled stack of faggots and logs was a grand play place, and the twigs smelt sweet and clean as the woods they came from.

There was a time when the Doctor kept a horse, a bit of a roarer, in this stable, which had originally been a coach-house; the one small stall adjoining having been adapted to the uses of a surgery.

There was an old counter of dark mahogany, shelves of dusty bottles, and rows of drawers with mysterious glittering gold labels, Radd Quass, Cort Aurant, and Pet Nit, etc. If you wanted a cork for a fishing float it must be stolen from " Subera," and in another drawer, labelled " Rad Zinzib," were some pewter " squirts " like the one used by Billy Hawkins on the day so sadly remembered by little Tom Ingoldsby. There were gallon jars of Castor oil and Mist Sennae comp, a chest of carpenter's tools, bins of physic bottles and vials, an old-fashioned ewer and basin of white delft, and sundries of every kind, and over all and among everything the largest and thickest cobwebs ever seen. Nothing was allowed to be dusted for fear a bottle should be misplaced, or some other damage done. In summer a species of enormous brown moth abounded such as in Devonshire is called a Witch. The window was extremely small and shrouded by a sweet-water grape Vine, so that the door usually stood open while the Doctor did his dispensing, to give him some light to see by.

If Winifred interrupted him, his words were decidedly emphatic. If she cut her finger while whittling a new hoop stick out of the faggots, it was most convenient to know where to find a first-class cobweb for certain to stop the bleeding. A kitchen cut was covered at once with flour, brown sugar, or table salt, but for a garden cut a cobweb was the desideratum, though it was known that salt healed a wound quicker than any other remedy because it hurt so at first, but it also required some of the courage of the Spartan boy who stole the fox to use it.

Besides the bee hives under the eaves of the stable, there were others in a wooden shelter beneath the greengage tree. There was more room there, and some of the straw skeps had little hives above them, caps for virgin honey comb. The bees knew the children well, and they were seldom stung by them.

It was late May, early summer, every leaf fresh and green, no dust, and no unsightly rags. Dame Nature's *Fest kleid* direct from her dressmaker. The beech leaves had not yet lost the marks of their accordion pleating; some trees were dressed in satin and some in velvet, and some in homely worsted stuffs. The palmy horse chestnut's leaves had each a downward crease that showed the marks of their folding and packing, and the oaks were still golden and hung with brown tassels of bloom. The tarred fence at the end of the garden was blistered by the hot sun and the children's fingers were stained with the moist pitch.

Winifred was seated in the garden barrow, using it as a rustic armchair, with its wheel pointing skywards and the handles down on the gravel path. Her duty was to watch the bees. She was passing the time by ill-using one of the spreading horse chestnut leaves, stripping away the soft green tissues to leave a herring bone of the harder veins.

The horse chestnuts that overhung the fence of Highfield Park at the foot of the garden were an endless joy to the children. One end of the swing bar was nailed to a chestnut, a strong young tree that put forth its gummy buds and pleated leaves, and reared its tall spikes of ice-cream coloured flowers before any of its neighbours.

The children had not many toys bought at shops, but in

springtime the Doctor was expected to provide a constant supply of chestnut whistles. He was very clever in that way, and on many an evening might have been heard the rhythmic tap, tap, tapping, that almost sounded like a busy woodpecker near at hand. The sap flows free in Maytime, and with gentle blows, not unduly hurried and free from any sign of roughness, the bark of the slaty-grey horse chestnut branches was made to slide off in an uninjured cylinder, leaving the wood below white and smooth as ivory. The sharp knife amputated the sloped head of the embryo whistle, a slice was cut for the mouthpiece, a notch was made for an airhole in the outer skin of bark, and when this was slipped back into place all was complete. When blown, the new wood gave out sweet flute-like notes, something like the soft whistle of a blackbird. A good chestnut whistle should be about six inches long and at its lower end be decorated with a pattern of shields and dots, which are the markings of the knots on the branches whence next year's shoots will spring. They are like the arms of the Duchy of Cornwall. To make the flute note higher or lower the ivory piston was drawn in or out of the bark tube, and the weird sounds produced were often more like the soughing of wind on a January night, than the music of a May morning. It required patience to watch the bees; it was nearly mid-day, and very hot even in the shade of the house, the air was full of the drowsy sound of humming insects. Winifred felt drowsy herself, as she sat in the wheelbarrow, with the dinner bell by her side, and she glanced first at the hives and then at the elder bushes against the tarred fence. From one of the hives in the low shelter there depended a dark brown mass closely resembling a head of hair in a chenille net such as the Doctor's servant wore on Sundays. The City of Bees was alive with energy and overcrowded; it was only a matter of minutes, or moments, when the younger generation should flit to find quarters of their own.

The elder bushes by the fence were not old responsible trees like the " wedding bouquets " in the carrier's garden, guaranteed to produce so many gallons of rich wine for the Doctor's cellar annually, but straight, bold boys and girls of the " Elder Mother," each trying to add so many cubits to its stature in a single year.

The young elders were toy-trees as well as the big chestnuts, for the Doctor made pop-guns out of their pithy stems, and these lasted for weeks, whereas the whistles perished in a day with the drying and shrivelling of the young bark.

The border by the fence was a pithy border, " pithy and pawky " as they say in Scotland, elder above and Jerusalem artichokes below. It was possible to make most deceptive-looking candles out of artichoke pith. A neat white taper fitted into the silver candlestick on the dining-room mantelpiece, with a little wick made from a burnt match end was sure to deceive an elderly relation sooner or later, especially if he were in a hurry and had not on his spectacles. There would be many moments of fuming and fussing because the candle would not light, but it was all very wrong indeed, and it was better not to wait till the fraud was discovered, and perhaps as well to remember the new Tickle Toby over the picture of lilies and roses.

From time to time there was a wild buzzing as a few hundred bees rose from the ever-increasing swarm at the mouth of the hive, but it was a false alarm, and they settled again with the rest. Next door to the Doctor's house was a chapel, it had long narrow windows, the top of each opened as a ventilator. Bees frequently appear to swarm on a Sunday, on the principle apparently of the better the day the better the deed, and, shameful to say, it was a joy to Winifred to accompany a Sunday swarm with all the bell-ringing possible. On one occasion the Minister protested he had

Near "The Cock" at Bowes Farm.

been unduly disturbed while preaching. The Doctor was very grave and polite, "but," said he, "if the bees were to enter your windows, owing to our neglecting the sounds that cause them to settle, you might find it very awkward." The following Sunday the thermometer stood at 90 degrees in the shade, and as ill-luck would have it a small cast or second swarm left its parent hive, and the moment the first sound of a bell was heard every window of the chapel was suddenly and tightly closed, and so remained to the end of the " diet of worship " while the faithful were slowly roasted as in an oven inside.

Perhaps what they bore that day in this world may be deducted from what they were to go through, in Purgatory, in the next.

It was high noon. The shadow cast by the plum tree had got less and less, till at last, between the boughs, a brilliant shaft of sunshine fell full on the brown chenille net. The meshes appeared to widen and part, and with a roar of sound the mass of bees separated and rose in the air, circling and zig-zagging like a black snowstorm, black in the shadow, rich red brown in the sunshine, their flight so rapid, there appeared to be a network of long brown lines against the blue of the sky.

Winifred sprang from her seat and began a steady tang, tanging, of her bell. The sound brought the Mother to the doorstep, the Boy, with long fair curls upon his shoulders, rushed out into the garden, secure in the fact lessons were fairly over for the day. The maid came from the kitchen and the lad from the stable. The Grandmother mounted the ladder from her garden next door and looked over the wall. All was excitement and there was no Bee-Master, the Doctor was out! He had left careful directions where he might be found in case of emergency, and Bill was soon dispatched to let him know the bees were swarming, and that he was wanted at once.

At first they rose high in the air, the whole swarm drifting now in one direction, and then in another, in an apparently aimless way.

It was a breathless moment. Her Majesty the Queen Bee is an erratic lady, and it is impossible to say whether she will choose the highest bough of the greengage tree or the lowest of a black currant bush. If bees mass themselves upon a branch it is easy to shake them gently into a hive, but if a firm support is chosen, such as the post for the clothes line, they must be brushed into it, with the hair brush the maid uses for the stairs, and it is far more uncertain whether the queen in the centre of the swarm will be got safely in or not.

This was a very heavy swarm.

" A swarm of bees in May
Is worth a load of hay."

*i.e.*, between £2 and £3 at old time prices. It was late in the month, but the hot weather had come with a rush. The bees were believed to think that a storm was coming when they heard so much noise, and therefore would try to settle and protect the young Queen. Learned people tell us now that they are deaf, but we did not think so in the old days, when it was considered a duty to tell the bees of deaths, and births, and family events in general. Two bells were ringing a terribly discordant peal, and scattered drops of water were being splashed in the air from a painted American pail. A light shoot of the apple tree had already a bunch upon it like a black egg, which grew with incredible speed to the size of an orange, a cocoanut, a negro's head. The bough drooped lower and lower under the strain of the weight, then suddenly there was a sharp snap, and the branch hung broken from the tree, and with a roar of rage and panic the whole swarm was again in the air. Higher and higher they rose.

## WINCHMORE HILL.

They flew up the garden towards the house, over the stable roof. A procession in wild pursuit rushed after them, through to the front garden. Everything now depended on keeping the bees in sight. The children ran and shouted, ringing meanwhile a peal that might have roused the village, and the Mother came panting behind in a large garden sunbonnet, and armed with a bundle of barége of a purplish grey spotted with red, to be used as a bee veil, as she had a terror of stings.

The swarm must on no account be lost! It was a veritable bee hunt, across the road, across the fields. Bees travel in a bee-line, but the children scrambled through the rough fence at the back of the carrier's garden, and the Mother had to go round in the other direction to enter by the five-barred gate. The field was blossoming with buttercups and the hedges white with late hawthorn above and with fool's parsley beneath, the oak trees were still golden with spring foliage, masses of wood anemones, tall and white, were to be seen at the edge of the wood, still pretty to look at, but shabby to gather, and the fern was uncurling among the brambles on the bank of the boundary ditch.

It was hard work and hot work to keep the swarming bees in sight. Another field was crossed, then a rabbit-holed bank, and a timber fence, to the public footpath of the wood. The children scrambled over a high spile gate, into the most private part of the estate. Luckily it was not padlocked, or the Mother would have been hopelessly out of the hunt. She was already far behind them, and the rough road and brambles hindered her sorely; her low, flat shoes were full of grass seed and pebbles. Every briar on the way knew she was out of her element, and reminded her that when she was a child she did not race like a mad thing through the wild places of the earth, but solemnly trundled a wooden hoop in a lady-like manner in the garden of Trinity Square, or walked by the dark Tower Moat with her maid. Through bushes and brushwood they went for a quarter mile further, but Winifred had kept the bees in view, and in the shade the pace slackened; the cloud of insects lowered and circled round a holly bush, wreathed with a garland of flowering honeysuckle, the creamy yellow woodbine that loves the shade and has the rich perfume of the Azalea.

The holly grew in a mass of lily of the valley leaves; the wild lilies were shy bloomers, and it was always a triumph to pick three or four spikes of the sweet-scented blooms.

At last the swarm settled, and massed themselves round the grey trunk of the tree. The little Bee girl gently " rang them down," while the Mother rested on a bank of moss to get her breath. It was more than half-a-mile from home, and just dinner-time, but no one heeded that; the great question was, " Would the Doctor arrive in time to hive them before something started them off again?"

A full half-hour of anxiety was passed in the beautiful woodland. The cuckoo's note was almost ceaseless, and even in the noontide heat a thrush from time to time uttered his restless " Do be quick," " Be quick," " Do be quick," or a blackbird whistled plaintively among the undergrowth.

The Boy with the fair curls wandered happily in the Enchanted Forest of forbidden ground. No gamekeeper was to be feared or trespass board to be considered when following bees. Indeed, the head keeper himself, a severe-faced old man with a nose like an eagle's beak, appeared to inquire what was taking place, and retreated again, with a respectful " Good morning " to the Doctor's wife, carrying his old muzzle loader in the hollow of his arm and calling his dog to heel.

Presently a quick step was heard, running lightly over moss and dead twigs. It proved to be Bill, who had found his master half-way to the World's End. He reported

## WINCHMORE HILL.

breathlessly that the Doctor was coming with all the necessary paraphernalia for the taking of the swarm. The Mother started to meet him, and sent the lad home for a supply of bread and cheese and mutton sandwiches to feed the hungry children. Soon the Bee-Master arrived; not in his long frock coat and professional tall hat, but bareheaded and in his shirt sleeves, bearing the hive, the bee board, etc. The skep had been rubbed and brushed with a bunch of fresh green balm and other sweet herbs, and smeared inside with a modicum of honey, that the Queen Bee might rejoice in the smell thereof and be willing to accept her new residence. The Mother swathed herself, sunbonnet and all, in the grey barége, and with thick gloves on her hands prepared to hold up the hive for the Doctor to brush his bees into it. He wore no protection, being nearly stingproof.

Down came the humming crowd, and the Mother stood her ground gallantly, though her heart was in her mouth the whole time. The skep was very heavy, and gladly she gave it into the Master's hands while the bees buzzed around them both in an angry cloud. Quickly it was placed on the board, with small sticks under the straw edge so that no insects might be crushed by its weight. In a comparatively short time the busy multitude had crawled under the dome, and it was evident her Majesty was safely within. Soon all was quiet, except for a faint humming and a few lost bees flying around. A picnic lunch was eaten. The Doctor enjoyed a well-earned pipe, and went home to do his dispensing, but the bees could not be moved till the cool of the evening. So a long and happy afternoon was spent keeping guard over the hive. In the soft summer twilight, when the nightingales were singing as if their hearts would break, the Bee-Master returned, and a tired and happy party wandered home by way of the village, Winifred especially proud that she had not lost the bees, the finest swarm of the whole season.

## CHAPTER VIII.

## ROUND BY THE WORLD'S END.

"The World's End." The very name suggests the "Back of Beyond." To reach it the village was left by Church Hill. It was an April day, but as warm as summer, the young leaves on the lime trees at Uplands were still small, and bright apple-green. The lilac bushes were in bud, and the horse chestnut spikes little pagodas of unfulfilled promise. At this end of the village the cottages were more picturesque than commodious. There was one with its gable end to the road built half of brick and half of weather boarding, the wooden part being the upper storey. The floor of the bedroom was so uneven that a chair would not stand upon it, but was obliged to be laid upon the ground till needed. The Doctor spent all one night there on business connected with his kitchen garden, or to speak more definitely with his "parsley bed," and he had to sit upon the chair to keep it on its legs; to lay it down when he got up, and to pick it up again when he wanted to sit down! His patient's bed had half a brick under one leg to make it usably level. Further on, there was a most picturesque row of cottages standing at right angles to the street; they had all gay gardens: violets and wallflowers scented the air. There were coloured primroses, purple auriculas, and a few hyacinths. The house furthest from the road was a Dame's School, an infants' school, kept by old Miss Wiltshire and her niece, where small people were instructed in the three R's, and the little girls learned plain needlework and how to "mark" in cross-stitch on perforated cardboard.

## WINCHMORE HILL. 79

Next came the Friends' Meeting House, which was very holy ground, as George Fox had once preached there. On the left was Miss Barnes' house, which claimed to be the oldest in the village, and to have been standing long before Enfield Chase was enclosed. It had a large old-fashioned garden and small fields marching with the Wood. The Meeting House was once struck by lightning, though it was quite a low building. The Doctor was sheltering at the Post Office opposite the King's Head, and watching the storm, with Mr James Riley, the grocer, when suddenly they saw the lightning strike the Meeting House chimney, which fell with a crash. They hurried to the spot, and found the old caretaker and his wife seated one each side of their fireplace amidst the pile of bricks, mortar, dust, and soot, they were unhurt, but nearly unconscious. The Doctor was once fetched to Hill House, the next on the right, because some mysterious illness had attacked the old sow, her farrow of piglings, and all the poultry. There was no veterinary surgeon, except the cow doctor, nearer than Edmonton, and he was sometimes asked in a friendly way to visit a horse or dog that had met with an accident. When he arrived at Mrs Wadeson's he found the little pigs and poultry staggering about the yard, everyone of them hopelessly tipsy, and the old sow as drunk as a lord! There had been a great brewing of currant wine, and the lees, well-fermented and decidedly alcoholic, had been thrown upon the dunghill on which the inhabitants of the stye and of the hen roost had feasted riotously. He diagnosed their complaint, counselled patience, and in a few days all had completely recovered.

Further down the hill Winchmore Hill Church was passed, a brick edifice built about 1827 as a Chapel of Ease to the Parish Church of Edmonton. It is chiefly remarkable for its vast whitewashed ceiling, which appears to rest on crossway beams of oak. In reality these are all plaster work, painted and grained to resemble timbers; their great weight is dependent from the ceiling, instead of giving it any support whatever.

Opposite the church was a low-roofed cottage of gentility, with gardens and fields reaching to the brook in the valley. Stone Hall was built later in these fields, the building material being the stones of Old Blackfriars' Bridge. At the time the present bridge was built a lady was induced to buy the old material as a speculative investment, but it must have been a most unlucky venture, as the stones lay for many years in a field on Wade's Hill in the form of dead and petrified capital, before a purchaser was found to give even a low price for them. Below the church were the New Schools and a pretty house with a jessamine-covered verandah, in which lived a Quaker lady, Mirah N——, who took life very seriously. She once told the Doctor she had been "born an adult." He did not quite see how it could be the case, but, knowing Friend Mirah, he had to admit the possibility, as she was somewhat unlike any other of his acquaintances, and never could have been young. The low cottage standing high above the road, next door, was till 1859 the Village School, and later was used as a night school. It appears as if it might have accommodated some fifty children, if they sat close together, and it is not surprising it was deemed insufficient for the needs of the neighbourhood. At the bottom of the Church Hill there were more small houses with gardens of wallflowers, irises, and white and purple stocks. The first house by the brook had a wealth of double yellow daffadowndillys. The stream had its source in the lake in the Park adjoining the Wood, and once when a dam burst in a flood, the stream rushed through the valley, bringing down such numbers of carp and roach they were dipped out of the water with common buckets, and the field ditches were alive with them, so that they could be caught by hand. There was a curious form of speech in this part of North Middlesex, which confused the Valley with the Hill. For instance, when one had come down Church Hill to the brook, they always spoke of the opposite slope as " going up the other side of Church Hill," and the same thing with the next Valley—" down Cock Hill and up the other side of Cock Hill." To the inhabitants it seemed a natural form of expression, but was most perplexing to strangers.

The Model Farm, since called " Camelot," passed through many hands, and was an unlucky house, where much money was lost and none ever made. The Londoner when retiring from business has an obsession that he could make a good thing of a little farm, feeling himself so much cleverer than his country neighbours. Sad to say, he invariably loses all his savings, and it would be difficult to count how many had come hopelessly to grief at the pretty house on the hillside. At one time Brahminy cows were to be seen there, which were of great interest to the children of the Village.

A stretch of woodland blossoming with wild cherry trees formed the corner where the road on the Chase side turned towards Southgate. On the other side were hilly meadows with straggling hedges of blackthorn, with long white flower spikes; a footpath that led to the Allotment Gardens, and in the blue distance the Essex hills, the hills with the sea behind them, in the mind of Winifred, who also vaguely mixed them up with pictures she had seen of the Welsh Mountains, quite regardless of such minor matters as the points of the compass. Her ideas of the sea were that it was like a much larger edition of the pond on the green, circular, and surrounded by pollard willows. She had also heard of bathing machines, and imagined them to be large boats with a square trap-door in the bottom, through which the bather bobbed up and down in the water. It never occurred to her that the sea would rise through the hole, and her machine and herself find a watery grave.

Cock Hill is said to be a punning translation of gallus or gallow's hill, because one of the gibbets of Enfield Chase stood at this spot. Quite a large colony of houses were clustered round the " Chase Side Tavern " at the corner, some of them both ancient and picturesque.

The hills between the Tavern, and the fields on which Chaseville Park was afterwards built, were so steep that the valley resembled a half-opened book with the swiftly running streamlet in the fold of the binding. There were old houses, or rather cottages, all down one side of the road, and two or three more important dwellings on the opposite hillside. There was a mineral well here, so strongly impregnated with Epsom salts that in the early part of the last century it nearly led to Winchmore Hill becoming a fashionable Spa.

Winifred and the Boy with the fair curls were on their way to the World's End to gather cowslips. They grew in such quantities that the Grandmother sometimes made cowslip wine. It was always a delightful walk, and never more so than on such a day as this. As the ground rose, all houses were left behind, and at the summit a ragged barn and a field gate marked the entrance to a cart road leading to Oak Lodge, half a mile away, and a fine view was obtained towards Slades Hill and South Lodge. A lake might be seen far below, white at the margins with water crowfoot, that curious plant which has broad leaves to float on the surface, and another pattern finely cut as seaweed in the depths below. In summer it was a place for water lilies, yellow iris, and the rare and beautiful flowering rush, one of the most graceful wild flowers that exist. Before the houses of Chaseville Park or the great

## WINCHMORE HILL.

mansion of Eversley were thought of, much less built, the lane was a complete avenue of beeches and oaks meeting overhead, wide stretches of grass were on either side, deep ditches overgrown with brambles and dog rose bushes, rushes three feet long might be gathered for basket plaiting, and now and again squirrels might be seen running in a spiral course up some smooth beech trunk, or a weasel gliding snakelike across the road. In the field where Eversley stands was a large gravel pit and a considerable rabbit warren. At the further end of the lane, where the gates of the Fever Hospital are now, there was scarcely a habitation in sight, a gabled farm was on the opposite hillside, and above it, a landmark from all around, stood Enfield Windmill. It was marked on the Ordnance Map as "Lonesome Cot." The road turned to the left, and became wilder at every step. Blossoming furze made a golden mass above the crozier tops of the young brake fern, and blackthorn, bramble, and briars covered the roadsides, soon the land descended sharply to a farm gate and cottage on the right, and on the other side was a one-storey wooden house, a sort of settler's hut, glitteringly white with a very red roof and bright green window shutters. The dweller seemed to have a taste in plaster statues, and the goddess Minerva, painted a brilliant blue, presided over the garden. When these were past, the grass began to grow in the middle of the road thicker and greener at every step, till at last it was a mere turfy track winding steeply down the hill, to come to an abrupt termination at two five-barred gates. This was the World's End itself, and a very out-of-the-world place it was. Looking across the fields to the windmill and the water meadows in the valley, it could be seen that they were yellow with cowslips, such cowslips as one seldom sees, tall and thick-stemmed, with a head of bloom that was almost a cowslip ball in itself. Those were the "Cowslip Meadows," never to be forgotten. The larks, rising higher and higher, filled the air with song, the note of the cuckoo sounded from the apple orchard of the farm above, and the children wandered up and down the steep hillside filling their baskets with flowers. Then they went down to the water meadows by the deep bed of the stream; it was a picturesque rivulet and one of many moods; now it was flowing rapidly over its pebbly bottom; the deeper pools reflecting the blue sky and fleecy clouds of Spring. Shoals of minnows swarmed gaily under its banks, and where it broadened to a ford, so that the cattle could change their pasture, there were shallow pools full of frog's spawn and tadpoles. It follows a winding course for many miles, passing under the New River Aqueduct at Bush Hill [that wonderful piece of engineering that has stood the wear and tear of centuries], under a county bridge at the fatal gipsy hole, where more than one lad has lost his life bathing. It passes Bury Street, and flows ever on, widening out into the Wash of Edmonton, and eventually mingling its waters with the River Lea in the green marshes below the Essex Hills.

It was crossed in the fields by high wooden bridges on tall piles, and in winter the floods often rose so fiercely it overflowed its deep channel, making a lake of the meadowland and sometimes carrying away bridges, fences, and gates before its onward rush.

Then in dry, hot summers it would shrink to a mere trickle, a chain of shallow pools where the fish lay gasping, and a dozen stone loaches could be caught by the hand in as many minutes. Surely the Doctor was the only epicure who ever had a dish of fried loaches or " stoney roaches " as they were called locally, served as an appetising relish for his breakfast!

There were willows with their yellow and silvery palms

## WINCHMORE HILL.                                85

and blackthorn as thickly clustered as on a Japanese fan picture, grey-leaved alders, and later hawthorn and wild apple made a glory of its banks, and in the World's end meadows the cowslips were finer than anywhere else.

There was a steep path to the Windmill and the many-gabled Farm, but the children followed the stream to a moated mound they called the "Castle Mount." On its steep banks were wild primroses, and the moat held forget-me-nots, yellow irises and tall bullrushes in their season. There were coots and water hens, and the greenish-brown eggs of the wild duck might be found among the dead reeds at the water's edge.

No doubt there was a house at some time on the Mount, but no trace of brick-work remained. At Cheshunt where a large double moat marks the site of the ancient Nunnery of La Motte, there are picturesque blocks of red masonry, chequered with yellow and grey lichen and moss, and the place has a name and a history, but the Castle Mount is only marked upon maps as "moat," and no more is known. All is mystery. Who lived there, and when did they live? It must be long since any house stood there as the mound is covered with large trees. It could only be reached by a plank which was sometimes placed there by the farmer when he wished to shoot wild fowl or to cut wood.

But now the sun was sinking and it was time to be making for home. The baskets were heavy with flowers. The children crossed the stream on the trunk of a fallen willow, and again on a farm bridge of logs, and climbed the hill by the side of the young wheat to the lodge and gate opposite to Minerva Cottage. They kept to the upper road, past the gravel pit and past "the Chase" with its farmyard and footpath. It was then a long, low white house made of a row of cottages and containing seven staircases. Just below was Fillicap's Farm, a small square house with a natural Lychgate formed by a pollarded larch tree. There was a stackyard full of sweet smelling ricks of last year's hay and straw, and a cart was being loaded with trusses for market, to start at daybreak next morning. It was all the finest upland hay, far better than the rich looking growth of the marshes; the latter is full of rank weeds, while the former is rich in clover and the finer fodder grasses. The hill below Fillcap's Farm was so steep that when the Great Northern Railway was made a forty-foot embankment was needed, the roadway was raised and the high viaduct built to carry the line across the valley. At the bottom of the hill was a most lovely ford and a foot bridge; two streams met, and there was a pretty waterfall over a weir some three feet in height. When Winifred was a child she was sure it was exactly like the Falls of Niagara; she had a coloured picture from the " Illustrated London News " nailed up over her bed, with the American Falls in the foreground and the Horseshoe in the distance, garnished with a rainbow. They did not appear to her to be as high as her beloved cascade at the ford. The lane was winding and narrow with deep ditches full of rushes and overhanging hedges of May and Blackthorn. It was always known as Dogkennel Lane, although it was marked as Old Green Dragon Lane in maps; perhaps at some far past time there may have been hounds kennelled in its vicinity, but if so the record was lost. The old " Green Dragon " is said to have stood in the Green Lanes, where Dogkennel Lane joins Bush Hill. There is a lodge built over the ancient cellarage. A short distance from the ford stood a picturesque inn, " The Retreat." It was hardly more than a beershop, where the market garden labourers went for their " eleven o'clock and four o'clock." There were some tarred wooden cottages with high pitched roofs standing back in long gardens, where spring flowers and cabbages grew in indiscriminate luxuri-

## WINCHMORE HILL.

ance. Near the gate was a large bush of Lancashire yellow-top, as the small double yellow wallflower was called; and a mass of grey-green southernwood, which in Middlesex is called "old man," but in the West of England is known as "boy's love." "The Retreat" occupied a central position; on the north side of the road was a footpath through the fields to Enfield, while the entrance to the inn was in a gravelled alley called the Hagfields, which joined Dogkennel Lane with Vicarsmoor and the village. The Doctor heard a queer tale about this place when first he came to Winchmore Hill, which tells of primitive times. A labouring man told the story of himself. He was seated one night alone with the publican, drinking and smoking, when his wife came to fetch him home. His cottage was not far off, and she came more than once. At last, in sheer exasperation, the innkeeper threw an empty pewter pot at her as she leant scolding over the half-door which divided the bar parlour from the vine covered rustic porch. The mug struck the woman on the temple and she was killed upon the spot.

"It was a terrible accident," said her husband, when he told the tale, "but the Master behaved very handsome about it, he gave me five shillings and buried her in his own garden, so I was put to no expense over the funeral!"

The footpath was said to be haunted by the apparition of an old hag, and many people were afraid to make use of it after dark. There used to be five stiles to cross on the way. The children would not have been afraid to walk through it at midnight, and could not understand the London terror of a lonely road. Their Great-Aunt, who lived in Doctor's Commons under the shadow of the Dome of St. Paul's, when she was told there was no danger, "as she would not meet a soul all the way," answered, "that is just what would terrify me!" They raced along in spite of fatigue, scrambling over one stile, and through the next, and via a dry ditch round the side of the third. The sudden " moo " of an old cow who had lost her calf startled them for a moment, but at last they were in Vicarsmoor Lane and nearly home. The dusk was falling and the white mespilus and double blossomed apple showed a gleaming white against Tom Hood's house, a dear old place, grey fronted and bow windowed, and roofed with shingle tiles red, brown, and mossy. The house still stands but the east front, which was its oldest part, has been altered. In those days it had long dark passages, unexpected stairs, and mysterious cupboards disguised with wall paper. There were two enormous pollard elms by the carriage gate, and a large cherry tree in full blossom made a white mass against the after-glow in the south-eastern sky. Vicarsmoor was a quiet lane with a few large houses standing back in their gardens and grounds. There was some new yellow brick stabling with a clock tower. The clock had lately been brought from the Town Hall in the Borough. Presumably it was sold because it was past work, it kept most erratic time, and was only quoted as an authority by those who required a good excuse for unpunctuality.

A pair of mournful cypresses stood on guard at the gate of a house with a slated roof and a long verandah painted in alternate stripes of dark and light green. The old Miss Catchpoles, who made the mead, used to live there, and later a Mr Burbank, an artist. He painted Pussy so well that he became famous as " the cat painter." This he felt so humiliating, he left grimalkin severely alone and turned his attention entirely to lions. A great picture of Daniel in the Lions' Den was his chief work, but attracted no attention.

The cowslip gatherers toiled up the hill, past a group of ruinous weather-boarding buildings dropping to decay, and came in sight of a row of beautiful old houses with tiled roofs

## WINCHMORE HILL.

and dormer windows. The largest of them had a verandah covered with creepers, and at the garden gate stood a tall handsome old lady. There was a shout and a call of welcome, and the Grandmother received the cowslips and the children with a happy smile of greeting.

## CHAPTER IX.

### FORD'S GROVE COTTAGE.

In the new bookcase—it is not more than eighty or ninety years old—is a dear old friend of Winifred's, the pre-historic alphabet book of Peter Piper.

It begins "Andrew Airpump asked his aunt her ailment." A tattered and torn, patched and mended little book more than a century old, with hand-coloured prints and a mottled paper cover. When she first had it more than fifty years ago, Ford's Grove had tall untrimmed hawthorn hedges, trees meeting overhead, and broad grass and running water on either hand. It was called Busk's lane in those days.

Justice Busk lived at Ford's Grove House, and to Winifred's mind it would have been more suitable if Justice Ford had resided there, and his brother magistrate removed to Old Park. She always thought of Andrew Airpump, Billy Button, and the rest of the Peter Piper family as belonging to the old cottage beyond Busk's bridge, that Davy Doldrum had slept in one of the casemented attics when he dreamt he drove a dragon (The Green Dragon was not far off, with a lively portrait of the same), and Humphrey Hunchback caught his hundred hedgehogs in the garden and fields. The Indian image Inigo Impy itched to possess was among the parlour curios, and possibly Captain Crackskull had been a crony of Captain Tills.

Once upon a time, when Winifred had been a walk with the Doctor over "Williamses" bridge and round by the Oakapple Pond, they found the old merchant sailor leaning over the white gate of the cottage. He asked them in, and

## WINCHMORE HILL. 89

and dormer windows. The largest of them had a verandah covered with creepers, and at the garden gate stood a tall handsome old lady. There was a shout and a call of welcome, and the Grandmother received the cowslips and the children with a happy smile of greeting.

## CHAPTER IX.

### FORD'S GROVE COTTAGE.

In the new bookcase—it is not more than eighty or ninety years old—is a dear old friend of Winifred's, the pre-historic alphabet book of Peter Piper.

It begins " Andrew Airpump asked his aunt her ailment." A tattered and torn, patched and mended little book more than a century old, with hand-coloured prints and a mottled paper cover. When she first had it more than fifty years ago, Ford's Grove had tall untrimmed hawthorn hedges, trees meeting overhead, and broad grass and running water on either hand. It was called Busk's lane in those days.

Justice Busk lived at Ford's Grove House, and to Winifred's mind it would have been more suitable if Justice Ford had resided there, and his brother magistrate removed to Old Park. She always thought of Andrew Airpump, Billy Button, and the rest of the Peter Piper family as belonging to the old cottage beyond Busk's bridge, that Davy Doldrum had slept in one of the casemented attics when he dreamt he drove a dragon (The Green Dragon was not far off, with a lively portrait of the same), and Humphrey Hunchback caught his hundred hedgehogs in the garden and fields. The Indian image Inigo Impy itched to possess was among the parlour curios, and possibly Captain Crackskull had been a crony of Captain Tills.

Once upon a time, when Winifred had been a walk with the Doctor over " Williamses " bridge and round by the Oakapple Pond, they found the old merchant sailor leaning over the white gate of the cottage. He asked them in, and gave the little maid an old toy book of his own, and that was Peter Piper.

All walks with the Doctor were pleasant, and the oaks and elms made the lane green and shady. In the wide ditches were sticklebacks and frogspawn, and wonderful caddis-worms, housed in tiny pieces of stick or collections of little gravel stones. Water rats splashed and swam under the banks, and in places the mud was painted scarlet with masses of thread worms. An ivy-covered trunk which leaned across the road by the cottage gate was so picturesque that later an iron chain was put to support it, that it might not fall. In a heavy gale some trees were blown down, and the fallen trunks lay for long on the grass by the wayside. It was a favourite stroll for lovers and old folks in the summer evenings, and they mostly sat upon the logs to rest, and listen to the nightingales who sang rapturously in the snow-white hawthorns. Mrs Busk noted this, and in kindness placed a rough bench there when the trees were carted away, and ever since there have been rustic seats in Ford's Grove.

Captain Tills was a sweet-faced little old sailor man with a fresh colour and silver hair and whiskers. The path up to the house passed between gay flower borders sweet with white pinks and clove carnations, and backed by a long row of pink cabbage-rose bushes. Mrs Tills was a tall pleasant old lady, who might have stepped out of a picture as she stood in front of the ancient cottage, with its diamond-paned leaded windows and mossy roof of shingle tiles, every shade of rich red and brown, bright near the eaves with yellow patches of poor-man's-pepper, light green mosses, and huge rosettes of house-leeks. It all looked so peaceful, but sad trouble had visited it. The only son had been killed at the siege of Delhi, and his father never recovered from his loss. Under the great walnut tree in the garden he built a sort of cairn of stones, which, from the descriptions that had been sent him, he imagined resembled his son's grave in India. It was a curious erection with a stuffed bird perched on the top, and by his special wish the Doctor sketched it and painted a picture of it for him. Captain Tills used to sit by his shrine and meditate on all the mysteries. Why the young die and the old are left alive, and why a nation's rejoicing should so often mean a nation's mourning? The peace and quiet of the garden and fields comforted him with the healing it always brings to out-door folk. The walnut was a magnificent tree at the back of the house, grouped with oak and ash and a dark yew, whose ivy-girt trunk was surrounded by a rustic seat. There were weather-boarding barns and outhouses with tiled roofs, and the vegetable garden was bordered by hedgerow elms.

Mrs Tills had two daughters; the eldest, Charlotte, though modest and retiring to a degree, was a clever woman, in many ways in advance of her time; the first girl in the Village to try and turn her talents to account and add to the slender income of the home. Mrs Todd of Uplands made it possible for her to attend the Female School of Art in Queen's Square, then quite a new departure, and twice weekly she journeyed to and from London by the omnibus, and worked very hard at drawing and designing. She won several medals, especially for designs for lace. That was not a time when girls might have studios and study in peace—all she did at home was hindered and trammelled by the life of the family. She sketched and painted in the parlour, and it was full of difficulty, as while she was drawing a bunch of grapes the Captain would be helping himself to "just one more," till what children call her "copy" had almost ceased to exist.

Ellen, the younger daughter, was sadly deformed, a

careless servant had left her on the top of a chest of drawers when an infant, and the result had been a fall, causing paralysis, which crippled her for life; but in spite of one arm being cramped close to her body, she was a marvellous needlewoman, knitting the bags and purses of microscopic beads that have been so much imitated of late, and netting fine silk purses.

The Doctor always used a long silk purse, and the mother made them for him, but her netting was not so fine as that of poor Nelly Tills. Both she and Charlotte excelled in Irish crochet, making the finest rose point lace collars for sale. The death of their soldier brother was a bitter grief to his sisters. The Mutiny was not a history book story in those days, but a horror of yesterday, even wiping the sufferings and terrors of the Crimea off the slate.

Captain Tills died early in the sixties. Not long after, his wife followed him, and Ellen, who had always been an invalid, died a few days after her mother, so Charlotte was left in the old cottage to face the world alone. I do not think she had a relation in the world. She took up her life bravely with such pupils as the Village could give her, and was an excellent teacher, endowed with endless patience and good temper. Winifred at ten years old became one of her pupils, and many a happy hour she spent at Ford's Grove Cottage. Two of the Vicar, Mr Frost's daughters, and some others used to meet on Saturday mornings for the lesson. Winifred must often have been a trial of patience, as she usually arrived breathless and dirty, having made a bee line across Highfield Park over muddy fields and mossy walls, but she was sent to wash and never scolded, and worked for the love of it to make up.

When Miss Tills removed in 1871 to the low white house on the north side of the Pond, which had been Miss Watkin's and later Miss Tebb's school, the cottage was taken by Mortiboy, the cow-keeper, and became very different from what it had been with the old furniture, china, silver, and curios of its former in-dwellers. Gradually it fell into worse and worse repair, suffering the decay of old age and neglect.

One of the people always to be seen in the lane was Ned Mitcham, Mr Busk's cowman. He appears in numbers of the Doctor's sketches in company with the Ford's Grove donkey cart. When the Doctor first came to the Village, Mrs Mitcham, his mother, was still alive, and she described her three sons as "One what worked, one what kept hisself clean, and one what did neither." Ned was the one what worked, and he certainly did not fulfil the other condition.

In its long existence the old cottage must have seen many changes and had many tenants. Some people date it so far back that those who dwelt there may have seen the marvel of the making of the New River, and viewed it as we now regard such innovations as wireless telegraphy and aeroplanes, or as the inhabitants of the old Village looked on the coming of the railway or the lighting of their roads with gas. When Winifred's great-grandfather had been from Maidstone to London and seen a short length of street lit with coal gas as an experiment, he came home saying:— "It was a pretty toy, but could never be any practical use." How little we know what changes may come in fifty years, and how strange would Winchmore Hill to-day appear to those who dwelt in Ford's Grove Cottage when it was first built. Did Billy Button live there who bought a buttered biscuit? and where did he buy it? at a shop that was the forerunner of Mrs Binsted's or Water's? Was it in some war-time famine that Enoch Elkrigg was reduced to eating an empty egg-shell? Who can tell us?

## WINCHMORE HILL.

" A fameless house of nameless men,
   A backwater upon the tide
Of Life, the house was once a home
   By love and friendship sanctified.

And when I see an ancient house
   In summer sun or wintry rime,
I feel amid the present peace
   The mystery of the olden time."

## CHAPTER X.

## SOME FORMER INHABITANTS.

The quaint dress of the Sisters of the Society of Friends was a familiar sight in the Village in the old days, but the only Brothers who wore the garb were Charles and William Brett of Suburban House. They were a remarkable couple. The elder a tall, gaunt figure, and the younger very short. They were clean shaved and oddly underhung in the lower jaw. They wore long dark brown coats, with knee-breeches, white stockings, buckled shoes, and shovel hats, and long white aprons with bibs tied round their waists. The apron had nothing to do with the Quaker garb, but belonged to their former trade of hardware merchants in Birmingham. Curiously enough, in the Midlands an apron is or was called a " brat," and Mr Willie Brett used to say their family name had the same derivation from a brat, or banner. Charlie Brett, as he was familiarly called, died when Winifred was a very little girl, leaving, it was said, £40,000. She used to accompany her grandmother to Suburban House to pay her rent, and especially enjoyed seeing a very clever grey parrot. Whenever Polly saw money being handled she used solemnly to remark, " Succession duty *must* be paid," and there was no doubt she had learnt the phrase in consequence of the number of times the family lawyer had been heard to repeat it. She always received her wages of a shilling every Saturday night, and gave no one any peace till it was given to her. When Willie became an old man he did not always attend to his toilet as carefully as he might have done, and the mistress of Rose Cottage told the Grandmother, " She really could not go to his house again till he put up his phylacteries." Winifred knew that the high flight of stone steps presented difficulties to the gouty feet of both old ladies, as there was no side rail to help them up, and for many years she believed phylactery to be a form of ornamental iron railing.

Two nieces kept house for the old man, and a nephew was sometimes with them, whose name was Jabez. The Grandmother showed him some kindness, in return for which one winter evening an unexpected visitor came to her door, who introduced himself by saying, "I am Jabez's father, and I have brought thee a pork pie," and an excellent pie it proved to be.

North Villa was for many years tenanted by Friends, and old Mrs D. was much attached to the Doctor. She was a strict teetotaler, but he was obliged to insist on her taking a drop of comfort at night, and she was so afraid her grandchildren should guess her evil habits that some of his best Cognac was sent to her every now and then in a physic bottle duly labelled, "To be taken at bed-time."

On one occasion he had the misfortune to send her a dead fly in some ointment, and she returned it to him with a Biblical reference written on the paper, Eccles. x., verse 1.

When about eighty years of age she removed to Tottenham, and one day her son was much surprised to receive at his London office the following mysterious telegram :— "Come at once; your mother has had another child." The word should have been "chill."

An important building near North Villa was 'Beadle's Warehouse. Few people would care now-a-days to store their valuables in such a Pantechnicon, a large barn of white painted weather boarding some 20 or 30 feet high to the ridge pole of its steep tiled roof. It was crammed from end to end with old and new furniture, carpets, etc. It was burnt down in March, 1878, and one lady lost the whole of her fine old furniture and quantities of beautiful china which had been stored there during her absence in Canada. Three villas occupy the site of the great barn, and one of the worst fires in the Village took place a few years ago on the same spot. Beadle's Warehouse was burnt on a brilliantly moonlight night, and the Doctor much deplored such a splendid bonfire being wasted. It would have been so much grander in pitch darkness.

Mr Wade of Beaumont Lodge, whose name is perpetuated in Wade's Hill, walked nearly every day through the Wood. If the wind was south or west he went by the sheltered footpath, down Southgate Lane, and home up Hoppers Road with the wind behind him. If it was north or east he reversed the process, that the trees of the Wood might break the keen blast from the Essex marshes.

A strange figure to be met in Hoppers Road was Mrs Lingard, who dressed entirely in the fashions of the Waterloo year—a clinging skirt of white or some light colour, a wide bonnet covered by a veil which hung far down below her shoulders, and an enormous muff reaching above her elbows. She was an extraordinary spectacle in the days of huge crinolines, and when bonnets and muffs alike were as diminutive as possible. Her white stockings and thin sandalled shoes were most unsuited to the rough gravel paths of those days. Mrs Lingard lived with her niece in Verandah Cottage, the only house of any importance on the west side of Hoppers Road. It was said her husband and son had been drowned together in a shipwreck, and her mind had stood still from that moment. She was harmless, unless any reference was made to Queen Victoria, for whom she evinced a great dislike.

At Woodside House there lived and died a Mr Neville, the son of the unfortunate Bellingham, who in a fit of insanity shot Spencer Percival and was hung for it. Mr Neville took his mother's surname, and tried to live down the terrible disgrace in the solitude of a country village. Trouble, and perhaps some hereditary taint, had rendered him melancholy and eccentric, and he was a pathetic figure in his utter loneliness and despair. He died from sleeping in a room with a charcoal stove, perhaps he could endure his life no longer.

It is true that " all houses wherein men have lived and died are haunted houses," but surely, as they say in the west country, spirits " walk." The old roads, even among new houses, tram lines, shops, and motor 'buses, have here and there an unchanged corner, a few trees, or a waypost that recalls vividly the personality of those who passed up and down them on business or pleasure in the days of long ago.

## CHAPTER XI.
## CHIEFLY HISTORICAL.

In an old Charter relating to Fairs in the Parish of Edmonton it is directed that "Beggarsbush Fair," which had been held near the King's Head at Winchmore Hill from the time of King Edward III., should in future be held between the Edmonton Church and Fillcaps Gate. This latter was the name of one of the gates to Enfield Chase, which was at the top of Bush Hill, near the house now called Elmscott. No doubt Bush Hill takes its name from the Fair. The etymology of the name Winchmore Hill is very doubtful; it is said that at one time there was a winch and windlass to Vicarsmoor Well, and that was the origin; but this well was sunk in the 17th century by a vicar of Edmonton, to give water to his parishioners on the Moor; and the village was known by its present title full three hundred years earlier.

In 1850 the pump near the pond on the green was erected at the expense of Mrs Todd, of Uplands; previously there was an open well there also which may have had a windlass. A child who was drawing water fell in, and was drowned, and the charitable widow had the well covered at her own expense so that such an accident might never happen again. The Vicarsmoor well was of no great depth, but the water practically never failed; it was usually within six or eight feet of the surface, and it had probably always been a mere dipping well.

A far more likely derivation is from the *Moor*, on which the *Whin* or Furze grew plentifully—The Whinsmoor Hill. It is more than a century since the enclosure of the various

## WINCHMORE HILL. 101

common-fields of Edmonton and Enfield Chase, and they must have amounted to about a third of the whole district. All the land to the North, roughly speaking, of a line drawn from Fillcaps Farm to the "Bell" at Scotland Corner, Southgate, formed part of the Royal Chase of Enfield, 1000 acres of which, on its enclosure, were allotted to Edmonton parish, in lieu of common rights, and were divided, *pro rata*, among the freeholders.

Enfield Chase became Royal property and a portion of the Duchy of Lancaster, through Mary Bohun, wife of Henry, son of John of Gaunt, Duke of Lancaster, who afterwards became Henry IV. It is said that the original Manor House of the Mandevilles, Earls of Essex, from whom the Bohuns, Earls of Hereford, obtained the property, stood in Trent Park, about a mile north of Mr Bevan's house, near the Hadley Road. The spot is known as Camlet Moat; there is a large moat, a well, and some remains of masonry. The memory of the Bohuns is retained in the name of Bohun Lodge, at the corner of Cat Hill, Southgate, and the road from Hadley Church to the Chase Farm Schools, on the Ridgeway at Enfield, is called the Camlet Way. The Grovelands Estate, Winchmore Hill Wood and the Park, about 300 acres of land, remains, probably even now, somewhat similar in appearance to what it was centuries ago, when it was only a portion of the primeval forest of North Middlesex. The "Great Forest of Waltham," as it was called in the thirteenth century, extended as far West as Harrow Weald; South, to Tottenham and Hornsey Woods; North, nearly to Hertford; and East, half-way across Essex. Forest, of course, does not imply continuous woodland here, any more than in Dartmoor or the Highlands of Scotland; but no doubt much of this wild country north of London was richly timbered.

Hornsey Wood has disappeared, and even a century

since was very small, as it occupied only a portion of the present Finsbury Park. Tottenham Wood has also quite vanished. It extended from Wood Green to the extreme western border of the old parish, near the " Orange Tree " at Colney Hatch; but Highgate Woods and Hadley Woods and Common, we have the satisfaction of knowing, are permanently preserved for the use of the people, as well as the beautiful forest of Epping. It seems a thousand pities that Winchmore Hill Wood is likely to be sold, sooner or later, in building plots. In the last fifty years the changes in the village have been enormous, but till the last decade they were slow and gradual. The rustic village has become a suburb; it is much to be hoped that it will not degenerate from a suburb to a slum, as has been the case with so many of the northern and north-eastern districts of London.

In the Sixties, communication with London had been considerably extended. There were then two omnibuses daily, making two journeys each way. The " Red 'Bus " went from the King's Head to the " Flower Pot " in Bishopsgate Street and the Bank, via Upper Edmonton and Stamford Hill; and the " Green 'Bus " from the " Green Dragon " to London Bridge, by Wood Green and the Green Lanes. This was the larger of the two vehicles and in bad weather had three horses. The journey was accomplished in fine weather in less than two hours, but half-an-hour late was of small consideration in those days. People whose business took them to the city daily, either drove the whole way in their own carriages, or walked, to and from, Edmonton, or Wood Green. At that time there were few houses between Winchmore Hill and the " Manor House " at Finsbury Park [then known as Hornsey Wood]. There were the " Dog and Duck " and a cluster of cottages in Hoppers Road, " The Fox " and a few houses at Hazelwood Lane, " The Cock " at Bowes Farm, " The Jolly Butchers," and

## WINCHMORE HILL. 103

a few shops and streets at Wood Green, which had grown up round the great Almshouses of the Bookbinders' and Fishmongers' Companies. At the corner of Hornsey Lane was the turnpike, where every vehicle had to pay a toll. Hornsey was then a beautiful old village clustered round its ivy-covered church. The " Queen's Head," a short distance further on, was a brand new red brick house, There were more dwellings after that, and the Northumberland House Lunatic Asylum, at the foot of Manor House Hill. Harringay Park was still a beautifully wooded private park and estate, and the Hog's Back, now Ferme Park, was only hilly fields. There was another turnpike at Enfield, exactly where the Village road in Bush Hill Park joins the London Road. The " Green Lanes " was a narrow road with broad grass down each side, it was only a gravelled way, and as there were no watercarts, the dust in summer was only equalled by the mud in winter. There was only *one* roadman in work for the whole district, Old Henny, who lived near the " Dog and Duck." His forerunner, named Scarborough, was a quaint figure, who wore an old tall hat and a smock frock. Henny worked also as a jobbing gardener, whenever he chose to consider the roads did not require his labours. When new gravel was laid extra men were employed, but it was simply shot from a cart and roughly spread with a spade, so Highway expenses were not large.

The Tottenham Gas Company laid a small main in 1864, but there was no public lighting till some fifteen years later.

There was no attempt at general drainage till 1873, and for the first five years it did little except pollute the shallow surface wells which formed practically the whole water supply. There were a few deep wells in the chalk, and the well at Eversley, sunk by the late Mr Wigan, when he built his house in 1865, was 360 feet deep. It passed through the chalk and gault, and obtained a small and fairly regular supply from the Upper Green Sand. Most of the cottages had no supply except from rain water butts, and they fetched their drinking water either from the pump on the Green or Vicarsmoor Well.

Winchmore Hill Church was consecrated by Bishop Howley in 1828. In 1844 some thieves broke in to steal the Altar Cloths and Communion Plate, but fortunately the Silver had been removed to the Curate's house. They accidentally set fire to the Church, and the east end was much damaged. Mrs Todd, of Uplands, gave the carved Altar, Pulpit, and Reading Desks, that there might be no " hangings " to be stolen.

The Church was a Curacy (not in charge) and only a Chapel of Ease to Edmonton. Before it was built, All Saints' Parish Church, and the private Chapel of the Weld Family at Old Southgate, were the only churches in Edmonton parish. The Church was not, however, the earliest place of worship in Winchmore Hill. Some of the first Quakers, when driven out of London at the end of the seventeenth century, settled there, and there have always been a number of members of the Society of Friends in the neighbourhood. Their Meeting House is surrounded by a large cemetery, and is holy ground, as George Fox preached there.

In the early part of the nineteenth century there was a famous depôt for the sale of smuggled goods, kept by Mr and Mrs Udall. It appeared merely an ordinary village shop, and stood on the Green, opposite what is now called Rowan Tree House, and on the site of the present stables of " The Limes." Mrs Udall sold drapery on one side of the premises, and her husband grocery on the other. The contraband trade seems to have been carried on in the most open manner, and yet the Revenue officers never succeeded in discovering where the stock was hidden; French lace, gloves, brandy, schnapps, silks, tea, and tobacco were *all* sold,

## WINCHMORE HILL. 105

although most of the articles were prohibited, and the rest were liable to high duties.

These people were of Welsh extraction, and were the founders of what is now the Baptist Chapel in Vicarsmoor Lane. There was at first something special about their teaching, and the sect were called " Udallites," but this name has long since been forgotten. At one time their minister was an old man living in a cottage in Middle Lane near the gate of the cricket field. The congregation assembled for worship one Sabbath morning, but their minister did not appear; at last two of the elders were sent to discover the reason of his absence, and were greatly surprised to find him hoeing potatoes, having entirely forgotten the day of the week!

Before 1842 there was an Independent Chapel where Woodside Cottages now stand, and from the numbers of bones found of persons who had been buried in or near it, it is probable it stood there for a long period. It was succeeded by a Chapel in Hoppers Road, which was pulled down when the railway was made, and was eventually re-erected in Compton Lane, under the name of the Congregational Church. This used to be called Back Lane. Lawyer Compton, from whom it takes its name, lived on the south side of the road, about half way down. The house was pulled down after his death in or about 1840, its ground being added to Highfield Park. Mr Wade, from whom Wade's Hill takes its name, was a retired merchant tailor, who died in 1865 at Beaumont Lodge, now Avondale College. The old gentleman used to tell an amusing story about himself and a friend, another "snip," with whom, after he had retired from business, he visited Paris. They went to an hotel where English was spoken, and gave the orders to a waiter, who promptly replied "Toute-a-l'heure," and they were much surprised and rather offended that he should at once have discovered their trade, for they imagined that he had said "two tailleurs" when they had spoken to him.

There have not been many local celebrities at Winchmore Hill. The best known is Tom Hood, who dwelt at Rose Cottage, about 1828. A part of this house is very old, and a vague tradition asserts that Henry Cromwell, son of the Lord Protector, lived here for a time.

Sharon Turner, the historian, resided for some years at Percy Lodge.

Mr Patten, sen., the well-known R.A., lived at Hill House.

During the construction of the New River, Sir Hugh Middleton lived at Bush Hill House, then known as Red Ridge. The most difficult part of his task was the construction of a wooden trough, or aqueduct, across the valley to the south of Bush Hill. This trough was 650 feet in length and nearly 30 feet high, and was supported by trestles. In 1780 the Protestant rioters, led by Lord George Gordon, threatened to deprive London of water by the destruction of this aqueduct, and the military had to be called out for its protection. To prevent such a danger in the future an earthen embankment was made, and at the same time the roadway was raised nearly twenty feet. The earth required for the purpose was obtained by making large pieces of ornamental water in Bush Hill Park and in Chase Park, Enfield. The latter is now known as the Broad Water, and contributes much to the beauty of the footpath from Winchmore Hill to that town.

At the top of Bush Hill is a footpath which avoids the long bend of the high road. It used to pass slightly to the west of its present position and was known as "The Poet's Walk" or Stoney Alley. It passed under an avenue of

WINCHMORE HILL. 107

limes which met overhead, and on its left was a black and sullen looking pond. Towards the Enfield end there was a high red brick wall, overhung by ancient yew trees, which made it exceedingly dark at the close of the day. It was reputed to be haunted, and few people would go through it after dusk. The ghost was said to be a lady in full bridal costume, who appeared on the top of the wall, gave a piercing and unearthly shriek and vanished. After a time it transpired that a white peacock found the wall under the trees a pleasant roosting place, and when disturbed it uttered its unmelodious cry and flew away. The footpath through the Wood to Southgate enters Southgate Lane at Clappers Green, an extremely pretty group of old cottages. The road passes the Pound, leaving it and Bourne Hill on the right, and eventually winds downhill to " The Fox " in the Green Lanes, and is usually known as " Fox Lane." At some fifty yards beyond the Pound there is a gate and stile into the footpath across what are known as the " Cherry Tree Fields." This is really " Old Park " and part of the estate of the late Major Taylor, owner of Winchmore Hill Wood. The original name of Old Park was Culland's Grove. From the footpath a Cedar of Lebanon may be seen on the southern slope of the fields. At this spot a large house stood till about 1830, which belonged to Alderman Sir William Curtis, who was M.P. for the City of London and an early advocate of popular education. He said that instruction in the three R's, Reading, 'Riting, and 'Rithmetic, was the true panacea for all social evils. He was known as " Nosey " on account of the prodigious bottle nose which was his distinguishing feature. He was a banker, and is said to have saved England from the French by providing money and taking up Exchequer Bills when other financiers would not accept them. King George IV. always professed a great liking and respect for him, and on several occasions dined with him at Old Park. Sir William is said to have been an epicure of the true Aldermanic type. His kitchen was a show place, a large and lofty room round which ran a gallery so that his guests could whet their appetites by watching the preparation of the meal, and inhaling the savoury smells of the cooking. The memory of Sir William is still retained in the name Alderman's Hill, and the lodge and entrance gate of the Park may be seen near Palmer's Green Station.

Strictly speaking Old Park is in Southgate, not Winchmore Hill, the boundary being the road known as the Bourne.

In 1800 a common was enclosed which lay between Vicarsmoor Lane and Dog Kennel Lane, now called Old Green Dragon Lane. It was known as Hagfield or Hagstye field, on account of a witch who infested it on stormy nights with her proper accessories of a broomstick and a black cat! The right-of-way across the common was left as an enclosed footpath. In the sixties there were five stiles in it marking the field boundaries. This is still called Hagfields, and not long ago was strictly avoided after dark. The Clapfield Gates, now Wilson Street, had also a bad name. They were said to be haunted by a black bull.

In 1840 there was no Post Office at Winchmore Hill. Letters had to be taken to, or called for at, the Green Dragon, and an old Postwoman came there from Edmonton three times a week.

A telegraph wire was laid to the village through Southgate in 1870, but for some time the messages rarely exceeded three in number during the whole day. The messengers were chiefly employed delivering groceries. The advent of the railway in 1871 was, of course, the great modernising influence on the neighbourhood, but even this was a small matter at first, as there were only sixteen trains each way a day and four on Sundays, and the whole staff consisted of a stationmaster, a boy booking-clerk, two signalmen, and a lad porter, and for the first nine months there was no telegraph. Also there was only one theatre train in the week, and that on Friday nights. What would the present inhabitants of Winchmore Hill say if they had to face the prospect of walking back from Wood Green, or if they were at all extra late, walking home from Finsbury Park, if they went to the theatre or any London entertainment, on any other day of the week?

## CHAPTER XII.

## THE COMING OF THE RAILWAY.

For nearly a decade before its first sod was turned a railway through Winchmore Hill had been spoken of as a future contingency. "When the railway comes" and "If ever the railway comes" were phrases to be heard again and again. Various plans were discussed, but nothing came of them, and most people felt that they should not believe in it till they saw it.

The first Bill that was sent to Parliament proposed that the line should pass below the village much nearer to the Green Lanes than its present position, and there was from the beginning an idea of continuing the Great Northern Railway through Enfield to Hertford, and making the new route the main line for passenger traffic, as there would be fewer tunnels.

In the Summer of 1869, rather to the astonishment of the Village, there arrived a load of barrows, shovels, and tip trucks, and the Winchmore Hill section of the Enfield branch line was begun by the turning of sods in a large field in Vicarsmoor Lane, near the present Goods Station. In a few days rows of wooden huts arose, mushroom-like, and gangs of navvies were soon in full possession. The work was begun also at the Enfield and Wood Green ends. There were at that time no houses between Winchmore Hill and Wood Green, except the old cottages on or near the high road, Palmerston Villas, and a few gentlemen's houses in their own grounds, and no part of West Enfield was built with the exception of some large villas on the Ridge Way.

## WINCHMORE HILL.

The great business was the spanning of the deep valley between the village and the hills to the North. The summer was one of heat and drought, the stream was nearly dry, and the engineers took an entirely erroneous view of its capabilities : they did not realise the extent of the watershed from the hills on either side, and when the inhabitants described " lakes of flood water, and bridges washed away and piled one upon another " they were listened to in polite disbelief.

The soil was dug from a cutting in " Brett's Field " and tipped to form an embankment towards Fillcaps Farm, and soon quite an imposing appearance was made.

The pretty row of cottages where the Grandmother lived were pulled down, the great ash arbour ruthlessly destroyed, and the garden devastated : the holly hedge, dense as a wall, was grubbed up, scarcely anything remained but the tall yew and a golden-knob apple tree, which for years after blossomed and fruited, on the top of the cutting by Vicarsmoor Bridge. The lane was closed for traffic, and a notice board proclaimed, " This Road is stopped time the Bridge is being built."

After men and horses had laboured for some time a working engine was brought down called the " Fox."

The excavations were beautiful in colour, the London clay being a bright cobalt blue when first cut through, and changing with exposure to orange. There were strata of black and white flints and yellow gravel; the men's white slops and the red heaps of burnt ballast made vivid effects of light and shade and colour against the cloudless sky of that excessively hot summer. There were also dark wooden planks and shorings to add neutral tints, and when the engine came the glitter of brass and clouds of white steam were added to the landscape. On Sundays and holidays the men were, many of them, resplendent in scarlet or yellow or blue plush waistcoats and knee breeches.

It was not till the 1st of January, 1870, that the Doctor's house was given over to the invaders and he moved to Grove Lodge. It was then all deep snow, and the cutting was so close to the side of the house that the garden shrubs were constantly slipping over the edge and having to be brought back and replanted. A portion of the wall was built, but the frost got into the mortar and it fell almost immediately, so the garden became a thoroughfare for the navvies at their work.

There had been much fear in the village of annoyance from the horde of Yorkshire and Lincolnshire railway men brought into the village by Fairbank, the contractor; but on the whole their conduct was very orderly, and they can hardly be sufficiently commended for their behaviour in and near Grove Lodge. A noticeable figure was "Dandy" Ganger, a big north countryman, decorated with many large mother-of-pearl buttons and a big silver watch chain. He instantly checked all bad language in the neighbourhood of the Doctor's garden. Many of the navvies brought their food or their tea cans to be heated on the great kitchen range, and never once made themselves objectionable.

It had been intended to complete the line in 1870; and that date may be seen on the girders of the bridge, beneath Winchmore Hill Station, but many difficulties were met with in the five miles of line; there was a culvert for the great stream in the valley, which looked as if it would carry anything possible, but when the water rose in the winter it sapped the foundations and the arch cracked badly; the treacherous clay, "blue slipper," sank lower and lower, till what had been meant for a level line became a steep gradient; long after the line was opened the "slip," as it was called,

John Cresswell, aged 72. From a Photograph.

John Cresswell, aged 26. From a Crayon Drawing.

was so dangerous that every train slowed down to pass it, and many persons were afraid to travel by rail to Enfield. The hollow in the railway may easily be seen from Vicarsmoor Bridge or even the Station platform.

The working engines had each a voice of its own, so that it was easy to tell by ear which of them was passing with its load of trucks. " Fox " informed the world there was " such a hurry, such a hurry." Hunslet, a tank engine, that arrived much later on the scene, was particularly clear in her enunciation, informing all the world of her huffy temper, though I never heard she was ill to deal with as a worker—" I'm in a huff, I'm in a huff !" she puffed on her way along the line. " Progress," who laboured at the Wood Green end, proclaimed continually the name of the chief engineer—" Mr Claringbull, Mr Claringbull," she shouted with a strong accent on the last syllable. " Ferret " seldom left the Enfield portion of roadmaking, perhaps because everything was " such a heavy load, such a heavy load."

Besides the trouble caused by the wet clay in the valley, another delay was occasioned by the thoughtless action of a gentleman who moved the stumps in his kitchen garden, which marked the limit of the proposed railway, and by so doing caused the centre line, originally surveyed, to become incorrect. The secret was never divulged, but the mischief done was incalculable.

The skew bridge under Hoppers Road was a big piece of building. It is where the Doctor's house and garden stood, and for one or two years after it was built the cutting each summer was a forest of rose and carnation poppies at least three feet high; they revelled in a new soil and made gigantic blossoms in every shade of crimson, scarlet, white, purple, and grey.

Five men were killed by accident in making the five miles of railway. A man who sleeps on a ballast heap on a cold night never wakes, the fumes are as poisonous as those of a charcoal brazier, and this fatality occurred more than once, besides other mischances.

All through 1870 the navvies worked; clay and gravel were excavated, and tip trucks filled the valley at Bowes and the much deeper one below the Enfield hills. A viaduct was built over Dog Kennel Lane, and the roadway itself raised 20 feet, the streams were imprisoned in culverts, bridge after bridge was built, either to carry rail over road or road over rail, the five-arch bridge at Warren House Lane being really picturesque till it became surrounded by houses. A huge sustaining wall supported the Grove Lodge garden. Station and platforms were built, sections joined, and the temporary metals became continuous for the whole length of the branch. A foretaste of the convenience of a railway was gained now and again by the wild delight of a rush home on " The Fox." Once a lurid night-ride from Palmer's Green seemed faster than the " Flying Dutchman " itself, as the little engine bucketed along over the roughly laid lines, with no weight of trucks behind to steady it.

More ballast was burned to lay the permanent way, and heavy rails and cast-iron chairs began to take their places. Another winter was passed, and it was said the railway would be opened early in the year; then a definite date was given, the first of April! But the villagers had waited so long, they only laughed at the day named.

"Oh! yes, *the first of April!* No doubt!" but when notices were published they had perforce to believe.

It was the night of the 31st of March, 1871, the permanent way was completed, the station was finished and smelt strongly of fresh paint, everything was ready. It was late

## WINCHMORE HILL.

in the evening, all was very quiet, the familiar sound of the working engine and attendant trucks attracted no attention, but suddenly the village was startled by a loud explosion, a perfect volley of explosions!

Many people ran down to the bridge expecting to find some unlooked-for accident had occurred. It was the navvies celebrating their departure with their last train of trucks by a fusilade of fog-signals under the bridge and railway station!

And on All-Fools' Day, 1871, the first passenger train came through Winchmore Hill, and the little village developed into a Suburb of London Town.

# WINCHMORE HILL.

The following poem was written in the Autumn of 1888, and is the record of a ride from Tottenham to Winchmore Hill, *via* Whitehart Lane, Wolves Lane, Tilekiln Lane, Green Lanes, and Hoppers Road :—

### A LAY OF THE SUBURBS.

Homeward in the mellow twilight,
Clattering hoofs across the tramlines
Over bricks and over granite.
Past the laden market waggons
Journeying slowly to the City
From the fields and open country.

Through the crowd of eager faces,
Crowd of toiling men and women;
Hurrying homewards in the twilight.
Past the glare of many a tavern,
And the flicker of the street lamps
As the lamplighter wends onwards,
Lighting stars along the roadway,
Till the lamps get ever scarcer
Towards the fields and open country.

Past the dwellings of the wealthy
And the wretched meagre houses;
Past the mouths of filthy alleys,
Straying dogs and tramps and children,
Shops and stalls and costers' barrows;
Past the gaudy painted hoardings,
And the hissing tramway engines,
Clanging, whistling, snorting, steaming,
Towards the fields and open country.

## WINCHMORE HILL.

Under torn and smoky leafage,
Past conventicles and churches,
Midst the din of barrel organs
And the sounds of oaths and strivings,
And the yelping of the street curs,
To a turning from the highway,
Leading towards the peaceful country.

Past the railway and the station,
Echoing walls and echoing bridges,
To the welcome tread of gravel;
Past the windows of the College
With the Catherine Wheels above them,
And the studious girlish faces
Toiling in the lighted classrooms;
Onward in the deepening twilight
Towards the fields and open country.

Past some cottages with gardens,
Dahlias, clematis, and asters,
Red and white and purple asters;
And a mother with her baby,
Chatting with her neighbour kindly,
Fire-light shining through a doorway,
On the haze of Autumn twilight,
Making ghostly lights and shadows;
Then a row of London houses,
Gazing strangely at the hedge-rows,
Over cabbages and turnips,
Over fields and open country.

Now a farm and now a footpath
And a pond that shines like starlight
In the flickering evening shadows,
Till the town is far behind us,

## WINCHMORE HILL.

And we pass between the hedgerows,
See the brambles and the ragwort,
And the twisting of the mist-wreaths;
While the ringing of the gravel
Dies on turf beside the roadway,
Where the sheep and spotted cattle
Lift their heads and wander onward,
Wander in the open country.

In the distance, in the fog-land,
Shines a candle in a window,
While the light of day grows fainter
And the evening mists wax denser;
So, along the winding roadway
Here, a tile-kiln burning brightly,
There, some women tramping homewards,
Tramping wearily and slowly;
With a bundle and a baby,
Through the still and lonely country.

Clattering hoofs on dust and pebble;
Now again we reach a highway,
With a glowing road-side smithy
And a noisy glittering tavern;
Then we cross a dreamy river
Looking weird beneath the twilight,
Bearing water to the City,
To the slums, and dens, and hovels
Of the toilers in the smoke-land,
From the breezy healthful country.

Here are houses near together,
Here a wood and there a hay field,
On the outskirts of the village,
Scents of mignonette and roses,

## WINCHMORE HILL.

Floating on the breath of evening,
Borne from many a cottage garden;
Now we clatter through the village
To the welcome open gateway,
Hear the friendly words of welcome !
Welcome ! both for horse and rider ;
Welcome ! in the Autumn twilight
From our ride through town and country.